Delivering Instruction to Adult Learners

Third Edition

Dedication

The support and inspiration for this book comes from my wife Ruth and my children, David, Julie, and Adam. To them and to the memory of my parents I dedicate this book.

About the Author

Jeffrey A. Cantor is presently Provost, Pensacola Junior College, Pensacola, Florida. He has served in that position since August 2005. He is responsible for a campus serving 20,000 students annually. Previously he was Dean, Extended Studies and Workforce Education, at Norwalk Community College, Norwalk, Connecticut. His previous positions included serving as Director of Technical Education for the Virginia Community College System, Associate Professor, Adult, Secondary & Business Education with Lehman College, City University of New York, and Director of Training, DDL OMNI Engineering Corp. Cantor holds a Doctor of Philosophy degree in Educational Leadership from Florida State University. He has authored several books, including *Cooperative Education and Experiential Learning* (Wall & Emerson, Inc.) and *Cooperative Apprenticeships* (Technomic Publishing Corp.).

Delivering Instruction to Adult Learners

Third Edition

Jeffrey A. Cantor

Wall & Emerson, Inc.

Toronto, Ontario

Orders for this book should be sent to: The University of Toronto Press, 5201 Dufferin Street, Toronto, Ontario, M3H 5T8. By phone: 1-800-565-9523 (Canada & U.S.) or from Toronto, 416-667-7791. Fax: 1-800-221-9985 (Canada & U.S.) or 416-667-7832. Email: utpbooks.@utpress.utoronto.ca. EDI through Pubnet: SAN 115 1134.

Requests for examination copies or for permission to make copies of any part of this work should be sent to: Wall & Emerson, Inc., 21 Dale Avenue, Suite 533, Toronto, Ontario, Canada M4W 1K3. Fax or voice messages: (416) 352-5368. E-mail: wall@wallbooks.com. Web site: www.wallbooks.com

Cover Design: Alexander Wall

Library and Archives Canada Cataloguing in Publication:

Cantor, Jeffrey A.
    Delivering instruction to adult learners / Jeffrey A. Cantor. -- 3rd ed.

Includes bibliographical references and index.
ISBN 978-1-895131-24-6

    1. Effective teaching. 2. Adult learning. 3. Adult education. I. Title.

LB1027.C35 2008   374'.13   C2007-906378-0

Printed in Canada.

Table of Contents

Preface to the Third Edition

The third edition of *Delivering Instruction to Adult Learners* includes a new chapter on Internet-based instruction, Chapter 8, which has become an important addition to the tools of teaching in recent times, deserving of separate treatment in a separate chapter. The Internet is also the chief reason behind many of the minor revisions and emendations throughout the text in other chapters, as a source of information or readily available resources.

Preface to the Revised Edition

This revised edition of *Delivering Instruction to Adult Learners* recognizes the significant impact of computer technology on the instructional process. Chapters 5 and 10 have been expanded to include useful information for instructors using software and computers in the classroom.

Chapter 5 now discusses computer-based testing and software programs that facilitate the creation and administration of examinations and track student progress. They may also provide the instructors feedback on their effectiveness.

Chapter 10 explores new applications of electronic instructional technology designed to improve the delivery of instruction. Specific attention is given to computer-assisted instruction and technology in the classroom. The chapter reviews the various levels of electronic classrooms, multi-media training, GroupWare for teaching, video conferencing, computer-based training, applications software, E-mail, chat rooms, and the Internet.

Prologue

Congratulations! You have made an important decision—to share your talents, skills, and interests with others. As an instructor, you will have an opportunity to make contributions to others, and to your community. Training and development is a young profession which is just beginning to gain recognition as a specialized field—and one for which formal preparation is required. That is one reason why I chose to write this book. Another is my genuine excitement about the field. I am exhilarated at seeing new instructors begin to put theory into practice and to feel comfortable at the head of the class. I enjoy hearing from people as they succeed as seasoned instructors.

As a result of a national focus on worker competence, high quality training programs have become an imperative, especially for those workers in positions of public safety or trust. Events such as the disasters at Three Mile Island, Bhopol, Chernobol, and the accidents experienced by Amtrak in Chase, Maryland, and the oil spill at Prince Edward Island underscore the need for training to ensure worker competency. These issues of public safety and the need for workforce literacy have created growing opportunities for instructors within all kinds of organizations. These opportunities abound, as people seek out new educational and employment opportunities and as changes in workplace technology demand new and continuing education and training. These training opportunities exist in business and industrial settings, community and technical colleges, and in public and community education. Not to be overlooked are the various public service organizations, including police departments, corrections agencies, fire and emergency services, and public utilities, including nuclear powerplants and the military. All are initiating new training programs or expanding existing ones. My experience indicates that the only initial preparation often afforded the trainer, newly promoted from the "ranks," is "on-the-job training." This is especially true in community and technical colleges where a newly-hired person in the technologies or business and career areas is selected on the basis of technical competence, with little or no attention paid to the education of the trainer. Thus, a need exists for a user-friendly book for those newly assigned to adult education and training.

I find that new instructors often feel inundated with unfamiliar terminology, timelines, and deadlines for producing required instructional materials, including lesson plans. Fear or anxiety in meeting the learner for the first time is also a real problem. Procedures for addressing these issues, and planning for effective instruction will alleviate many of these concerns. As a new instructor, you initially may find the job rather mechanical with no latitude for flexibility, originality, creativity, or individual personality. But, the success of training depends upon your ability to use the available training tools and proven processes in an original, creative, and flexible manner, with a full understanding of the uniqueness of a specific situation and of the psychology of the learner. No tool, procedure, or guideline can be generated to take the place of this creative ability in each and every instructor. Nowhere else is this more important than in the presentation of instruction. The success of the training effort depends upon the effective use of your innate abilities, coupled with a systematic approach to developing and implementing instruction.

The instructor succeeds or fails in the classroom. Everything comes together in the classroom, where it becomes apparent whether or not you are fully prepared and capable of carrying out the instructional task. It is not enough to be effective in lesson presentation, but not prepared to work effectively with your learners. Alternatively, to be effective with your learners but not prepared to present the material is also unsatisfactory. In the classroom, you must be prepared and able with an extensive array of skills and knowledge. These include: knowledge of the instructional content; skill at efficiently presenting the material through the appropriate instructional media; awareness of each learner's needs and best learning style; basic understanding of adult learning theory; and effective use of interpersonal skills when addressing a broad spectrum of learner performance, attitudes, skill levels, and interests.

This text is designed and written to fulfil these objectives. It is dedicated to those special people, the instructors, adult educators or trainers, who have been left for so long to their own devices, and who fulfil a much needed role in society—that of educating tomorrow's leaders.

This book is designed to assist the new instructor or the seasoned professional by providing an easy-to-use set of tools for understanding the attributes, skills, and knowledge required for effective instruction. It is based upon processes and techniques used in training programs developed for highly critical skills training in the military and para-military (Fire and Emergency Medical Services) and nuclear utility industries. The book approaches the job of the instructor from a threefold perspective, including: the instructor as a professional; the needs of the learner; and the instructional process and related technology. It presents this information in a concise and graphic manner.

Chapter 1 describes and discusses the successful instructor, and the roles and responsibilities of an instructor, including professional preparation, personal characteristics, and maintenance of professional qualifications. It is based on an analysis of the technical and corporate training profession, and core competencies outlined in The American Society for Training and Development's *Models of Excellence Study*. It highlights those characteristics and professional attributes which combine to make a successful training professional, so as to provide a framework for understanding the job of the instructor and the areas in which a new instructor should become knowledgeable. Chapter 2 follows with a description of effective communication in the instructional setting.

Chapter 3, based on Gagné's learning theories, provides necessary information to lead to an understanding of the learner. The learning process is discussed. An overview of cognitive psychology and the principles of adult learning is included. With this better understanding, you, as an effective instructor, can begin to design successful instruction.

The book next discusses design and delivery of instruction. Chapters include instructional objective development, lesson plan development, methods of instruction, motivation, instructional evaluation, and management of the classroom environment.

The book is written in non-technical language and assumes no prior training in education, psychology, or related disciplines. Graphics supplement and complement the text. At the end of each chapter there is a list of references pertinent to the subject covered in the chapter. In addition there is a reference list for additional information and reading at the end of the book.

Good luck in your studies and pursuits.

1

The Effective Instructor as a Behavior Model and Change Agent

Your role as an instructor is to be a leader, helper, guide, change agent, coordinator, and facilitator of learning.

This book is designed to provide you with the essential information and knowledge to develop the personal attributes and professional behaviors necessary to become an effective instructor. This first chapter describes and discusses specific personal qualities that instructors should possess, as well as their professional roles and responsibilities, and culminates with ten principles to guide you in becoming an effective instructor, that is, a behavior model and change agent for your learners. A clear understanding of these personal attributes, roles, and responsibilities will assist you in accomplishing your instructional objectives while building your learners' self-esteem.

The basic principles for instructing adults described in this book are based upon the science of andragogy. This term, *andragogy*, refers to adult-centered education (Knowles, 1984). Whereas the Greek root words for pedagogy mean "leading children," andragogy means "leading adults."

What is an Instructor?

You are an adult responsible for instructing other adults. With the best of intentions, you wish to motivate and lead people to learn. Imagine for a moment that you are a learner in your own class. Do you, as a learner, like the way you, as an instructor, are teaching?

A Behavior Model

As an instructor you are often the first person in your organization or institution to establish contact with a learner. Learners tend to be in an impressionable state when they enter a new, unfamiliar learning environment. In such situations, they look for a behavior model, someone they can imitate and after whom they can pattern their new behavior (Rosenbaum & Baker, 1989, and as further underscored by King et al., 2001). Learners will watch and absorb the way you conduct yourself in the classroom and laboratory. They will keenly observe your mannerisms, speech, teaching style, and personal habits. The behavior model provided by an instructor will live on long after he or she leaves. Therefore the legacy must be as constructive and positive as possible.

A Change Agent

All instructors share a unique opportunity to act as "change agents," that is, someone who changes the behavior of others through the educational process. The concept and role of change agent is very important in the field of adult education and training. As an instructor of adults, your major responsibility is to instill a desired set of behaviors in your learners by providing guidance, support, direction, and suggestions. In your classes, you will discuss, demonstrate, critique, and sometimes lecture. Your learners will change as they learn new information and skills, new ways of behaving and acting: in other words, you will function as an agent for change with your learners.

How then, would you, as a learner, like to learn from you, as an instructor? How can you be an effective behavior model and change agent for your learners? You, as a learner, want to be in an exciting and intellectually stimulating learning environment. You need and want to acquire knowledge and skills that are interesting, as well as applicable to your real-world situation. You like to participate in activities and solve problems in a spirit of mutual inquiry. You expect to be treated with courtesy and respect. You wish to feel free to seek encouragement and assistance when necessary without being embarrassed or restricted. You require feedback and recognition for your contributions. You also need to judge your own progress. Therefore, you want your instructor to be a leader and facilitator, not merely a caretaker.

A Goal for Instructors

Make it your goal to instruct in ways you would want to be taught. Strive to be a leader—a catalyst and change agent in an atmosphere of informal and respectful collaboration. Your major responsibility is always to facilitate and encourage learning. Mutual planning and work carried out by you and your learners together should drive the learning process. First help your learners set goals for themselves, and then enable them to achieve them. Accept your learners as they are, and use their experiences and learning history as a foundation upon which to build. Recognize that the learning speed of each person will differ. If you allow enough time so that the individual learning needs of all learners are met, all can find learning satisfying. Help them succeed! Strive to reach the goal: "Teach unto others as you would have others teach unto you."

Attributes of an Effective Instructor

We can all recall one or more special instructors who have influenced us profoundly. To help you become an effective instructor, try to understand what made these people so special. Take a moment and think about those attributes or approaches that made one or more of your instructors so outstanding. Figure 1-1 displays some of your possible responses.

Attributes of an Effective Instructor

Possible Responses
- What qualities did this individual possess?
  - ☐ Patience
  - ☐ Kindness
  - ☐ Love of subject
  - ☐ Fairness
  - ☐ Was a good speaker
- What do you remember most about this person?
  - ☐ Good sense of humor
  - ☐ Knowledge of subject
  - ☐ Made subject understandable
  - ☐ Helped me
  - ☐ Answered my questions
  - ☐ Seemed to care

Figure 1-1. Source: National Fire Academy, *Instructional Methodology*, 1989.

Now let's take a closer look at what special attributes you, as an instructor, should bring to your adult learners. There are certain basic requirements we all must meet in order to teach.

- Instructors must care about their subject.
- They must have attained basic competence in their subject.
- They must want to share their knowledge.

In addition to these basic requirements, organizations such as the American Society for Training and Development (1983), U.S. Army Corps of Engineers (1982), National Fire Academy (1989), and others who sponsor training programs collectively cite several basic characteristics of effective instructors. Many of these characteristics are suggested by recent research

(Robbins, 1990; Kuchinke & Peter, 2000), and will be presented in the following sections.

Based on my four decades of instructional experience, I like to sum up what a successful instructor possesses this way: (1) knowledge of oneself; (2) knowledge of the learner; (3) knowledge of the subject; (4) knowledge of appropriate instructional techniques; and, (5) knowledge of administrative requirements and ethical responsibilities.

Knowledge of Oneself

You, as an effective instructor, must understand your motivation for being an instructor of adults. You must be aware of what it is you derive from teaching and what it is that you wish to accomplish. You must also be aware of your responsibilities to your firm or organization, as well as to the learners you will influence as a behavior model and change agent.

The first requirement of you as an instructor is that you have a strong sense of purpose. Each instructor must define his or her own goals. An instructor must select a target and zero in on it.

How do you, as an instructor, define your individual goals? One way is to ask a series of questions about the instructional assignment and how it fits into the big picture:

- What is the mission of the firm or organization?
- What is the purpose of training for the firm or organization?
- What is my relationship, as an instructor, to the mission of the firm or organization?
- For what aspects of the learners' learning am I responsible?
- How is the subject that I teach directly related to the actual job(s) my learners perform?

You must find valid answers to each of these questions; moreover, you should have the answers firmly in mind before teaching the first lesson.

Well-defined goals are of no value unless they are worthwhile. Make sure that yours are useful and important for both your learners and your organization. And finally, remember that some goals are unrealistic if they are beyond the capabilities of either you or your learners.

Knowledge of the Learner

To enhance the learning environment you must understand adult learning theory and be able to use motivational and group dynamics techniques. You also must carry out initial and ongoing audience analyses to ensure that your learners receive instruction tailored to their needs. And you must continue to learn more about them both as learners and as people throughout the training process.

Knowledge of the Subject

Draw upon your content knowledge and keep up to date with current data and future trends in your particular field. Never consider it sufficient to be one unit ahead of your learners.

Knowledge of Appropriate Instructional Techniques

You must utilize the best methods for preparing and presenting subject matter content. To help you in this regard is the fundamental purpose of this book. You must also be able to use the different media that can make content come alive.

Knowledge of Administrative Requirements and Ethical Responsibilities

You must be familiar with all essential organizational and administrative requirements (e.g. grading and returning exams, keeping attendance rolls, noting lesson plan revisions, etc.) and must fulfill these requirements in a punctual and professional manner. You should also understand and implement the various policies (e.g. safety, equal employment opportunity, etc.) of your firm or organization. Finally, you must understand where

A Code of Ethics for Instructors

- Seek and share truth.
- Govern behavior by ethically sound principles.
- Maintain high standards of professional integrity
- Recognize unique human personalities and strive to help each learner reach full potential.
- Deal impartially with all learners.
- Strive to broaden understanding and knowledge to become a better instructor and leader.
- Contribute to and loyally support the organization and its missions and standards.
- Be conscious of the privilege and responsibility to preserve and strengthen the integrity of the organization.

Figure 1-2.

you fit within the firm or organization's chain of command and appreciate your function as a change agent.

A typical firm or organization has standards of ethical conduct that build public confidence and create an atmosphere of mutual respect and solidarity within and outside that firm or organization. You must be aware of and implement these ethical standards through your training program. A sample Code of Ethics (from one organization in which I worked) is displayed in Figure 1-2.

You are responsible for dealing justly and impartially with your learners, regardless of their physical, mental, racial, or religious characteristics. You must also display integrity and loyalty to other members of the profession. Finally, you are to give wholehearted support to your programs.

Your Roles and Responsibilities as an Instructor

What separates an effective instructor from a competent technician or subject matter specialist? Having gained a knowledge of the requisite personal attributes and characteristics of instructors, another major step in the process of becoming an effective instructor is to become familiar with specific instructional roles and responsibilities, some of which are listed and then discussed below.

You Are a Professional

As a professional instructor, you will conform to your personal ethical standards, as well as those of your firm or organization. A typical firm and its training program should have standards in areas such as:

Training Program Operation	Technical Expertise
Instructional Expertise	Instructional Methodology
Instructor Demeanor	Classroom Etiquette
Evaluation	Planning and Scheduling
Housekeeping	Record Keeping

You, as a professional, are also responsible for understanding fully and supporting the standards that apply to your profession and suggesting changes to these standards as you see needs arise. In addition, you must implement those standards meticulously and consistently, remaining technically and instructionally proficient.

You Are a Leader

The word "education" comes from the Latin word *educare*, which is a combination of *e*, meaning "out," and *ducere*, "to lead." Ideally, education is a process by which a person is "led out" into a search for knowledge, deeper insights, and increased wisdom.

How do you lead learners? A good leader is able to inspire subordinates to make their best efforts. However, no effective leader actually does the subordinates' work for them. Instead, as an instructor, you lead, guide, direct, and point the way. It follows, therefore, that you must ensure that your learners put serious effort into the learning enterprise. Your learning goals can be reached most efficiently through the combined efforts of you and your learners.

In the final analysis, learners learn individually. After all, learning is change and growth that goes on within the individual. Each learner has unique drives, anxieties, frustrations, abilities, hopes, and potentialities. You face the challenge, responsibility, and opportunity to mold new personnel through your instructional leadership.

You Are Well Prepared to Instruct

Making errors in the classroom, such as imparting inaccurate information, relying on tired, out-of-date notes, making a poor presentation, or having an indifferent or unpleasant manner, can adversely affect the attitude and behavior of the learners in the classroom and their performance on the job. In addition, your credibility and/or that of the training program can be tarnished. For this reason, you must be well prepared. This includes:

- knowing and understanding the material to be taught;
- understanding applicable learning theory, including awareness of learners' needs, attitudes, motivation, and ability;
- being completely familiar with the instructional systems approach to the design and development of instruction;
- organizing the instructional format and setting; and,
- being emotionally and psychologically ready to cope with learner needs.

As well as knowing your subject and how to teach it, skill in dealing with people is essential in order for you to be an effective instructor. Therefore, you must:

- demonstrate genuine concern for and interest in participants' progress and well-being;
- continue to find out more about learners' abilities and encourage learners to improve on and develop their strengths;
- work one-to-one with individual learners as needed; and,
- approach the learning situation with enthusiasm and good humor in order to create a positive learning environment.

You Establish Mutual Trust

Your firm or organization entrusts you with the responsibility for determining whether or not a learner has sufficiently mastered certain skills and knowledge. Standards of performance established in each training program must be met as part of a learner's qualification to undertake a specified job function. The organization trusts that you will not recommend anyone who has not mastered the required skills and knowledge.

A second trust, an educational trust, is given by the learners to you, as the instructor. Their trust is that you will prepare them to perform the job properly, thus demonstrating care for and interest in them.

Thus, your foremost responsibility is to maintain the organization's standards and to pass or recommend only those learners who meet those standards. Your next responsibility is to help the learners understand the required material and master the appropriate skills. This dual accountability puts a heavy burden of responsibility upon you. You must preserve a teaching/learning relationship with the learners and, at the same time, maintain organizational standards. You must be supportive, but never suggest that shortcuts around or lowering of the standards are permissible.

To further compound the issue of trust, while you are an instructor, you are also an employee of the organization, and must, from time to time, also become a fellow learner alongside others who earlier may have been instructed by you.

These three roles may appear to be in conflict, but they are not. In fact, they offer a perfect opportunity for an instructor to model proper job-related behavior in a complex situation. When learners assume their jobs in the work environment, they will be required to respond to similar role conflicts on the job. They may very well work with or for people with whom they become friends. Unfortunately, in certain situations, these people may ask their fellow workers to compromise the standards or bend the rules. The reasons for suggesting such deviations usually are compelling to those who ask: they may not have enough time to finish the job properly or may want to cover up an error. No matter what the reason, a request to ignore a standard must be denied. The person involved must be encouraged to correct and/or avoid the deviation before it becomes a serious safety concern and/or a possible legal problem. The incident even may have to be reported to management.

Similarly, every instructor at some point encounters a learner who seems responsible and knowledgeable in class discussions, but who consistently fails. You, as an instructor, have a feeling that the person should be able to qualify for this job, yet he or she is unable to do the work. In this case, you are doubly accountable. First, you must uphold the standards by not passing the learner. Second, you must meet with such learners and attempt to find ways to improve their performance.

Obviously, the learner should be provided with guidance and help. You have a responsibility to facilitate and support each learner's attempt to master the material, but must also establish a clear understanding that the standards will not be lowered. The learner must then heed the advice and seek the suggested help.

You Establish Credibility

Credibility is based on the faith that one person (the learner) places in another person (the instructor) after reasonable grounds for such trust have been established. This trust occurs when the stated ideals and actual practices of the instructor are consistent. Credibility is difficult to earn and easy to lose. You, as an instructor, must establish and maintain your own credibility and the credibility of the organization.

Sometimes a single, seemingly insignificant event can destroy your credibility as an instructor. For example, punctuality is a sign of a highly professional operation. Lack of punctuality suggests that the operation is less than professional and, therefore, is not credible. It is not businesslike for a class, scheduled to start at 8 a.m., to start 15 or 20 minutes past the hour. If people leave 5, 10, or 15 minutes or more before the end of their scheduled workday, credibility is damaged. If lunch is to end at 1:00, and yet the next class does not start until 1:15, again, credibility is damaged.

Any lack of professionalism in the classroom can severely damage credibility. You must establish high professional standards for yourself and also demand high standards of professionalism from the learners. Negative attitudes, feet on the tables, leaving the classroom messy, intentionally damaging company property, sloppy dress standards, and lack of respect for others are all specific examples of a lack of professionalism.

Never minimize the significance of credibility—seemingly small events can have a very destructive impact on both your credibility and that of the organization. You need to earn the reputation as a highly professional individual in order to instruct effectively. The training organization shares both the positive and negative reputation of its instructors.

Ten Principles for Instructing Adults Effectively

- Act as a leader, helper, guide, change agent, coordinator, and facilitator of learning.
- Promote active participation and three-way communication.
- Recognize the individuality of the learner.
- Assist your learners to set and understand goals.
- Use effective questioning.
- Be experience-centered.
- Encourage mutual problem-solving.
- Be a group member yourself.
- Reinforce learning through self-evaluation.
- Develop a collaborative climate.

Figure 1-3.

Ten Principles for Instructing Adults Effectively

Throughout this chapter I have described the role of an effective instructor as change agent and behavior model. I have outlined the necessary attributes and characteristics and the various roles and responsibilities of an instructor. Ten basic principles for instructing adults now emerge to guide you through the text material. Figure 1-3 displays these ten principles. Let's look more closely at them, as the remainder of this book will discuss and reinforce these principles of adult learning.

Understand Your Role as an Instructor

This chapter described you, the instructor, as a leader, a helper, a guide, a change agent, a coordinator, and a facilitator of learning. Suppose you are a learner in the kind of class where the main reason to learn is so you can pass the test.

You are required to memorize and repeat whatever the instructor wants. You would like to explore a couple of topics more deeply on your own, but get no help (and perhaps even discouragement) from the instructor. How do you like it? Enough said! The chapters on the development of instructional objectives, lesson planning, instructional methodologies, etc., will provide insights into how best to facilitate the learning process.

Promote Active Participation

Encourage active participation and three-way communication. Imagine that you are a learner in a class where the instructor lectures for the whole period and then, at the last minute, asks if there are any questions. A learning activity that breaks you into small discussion groups or otherwise involves all learners is never used. The communication is almost always all one-way. What do you think? The chapters on communication and on instructional evaluation and test development will deal with these situations.

Recognize Your Learners' Individuality

Recognize that while learning abilities differ, as a person each learner has the same worth and is entitled to the same respect. Suppose you are a learner in a class where the instructor caters to the fastest learners. You are having some trouble with a couple of things and feel somewhat unable to cope and behind the rest of the class. There are others in the same boat, and you are all sinking from the lack of a helping hand. You can tell the instructor thinks less of you than some other learners. How do you feel? The chapter on adult learning and motivation and learned helplessness will provide you with some insights on how to accommodate all learners' needs.

Assist Your Learners to Set Clearly Understood Goals

Help your learners set goals for themselves and understand the need for what they must learn. Picture yourself in a class where the instructor determines what, when, and how everything is to be learned. Almost like elementary school isn't it? The teacher dominates, and you are placed in a dependent position. You are not helped to understand "why." You are just told to do it. How do you like it? The chapters on adult learning, writing and using learning objectives, and motivation will demonstrate why it is necessary to involve your learner in the learning process right from the beginning.

Use Effective Questioning

Ask probing, higher level questions to promote independent thought. Picture yourself as a learner in a class where the instructor never makes you think. Very few questions are ever asked, and those are low-level questions on factual material only. You are not challenged and never given the opportunity to analyze and synthesize. There seems to be no spirit of inquiry and no exploration of creative relationships. How do you respond? The chapters on instructional objectives and communication techniques will describe how to use questioning effectively to promote learning.

Be Experience-Centered

Use learner experiences to help teach. Suppose you are a learner in a class where you are never asked to share your background experiences and knowledge about the task. You know that everyone has at least a little experience, and some people have acquired a lot of information. The instructor, however, never takes the time or effort to discover this, only seems interested in sending information and experiences your way, and looks for none in return. How do you react? The chapters on communication, motivation, and instructional methods will share information on how to capitalize on learner experiences.

Encourage Mutual Problem Solving

Take a mutual problem-solving or task approach to impart knowledge that has application to the job. Suppose you are a learner in a class where the purpose seems to be to learn things of no apparent relevance to your job or interests. The instructor insists that it may be of value to you someday. Do you enjoy this kind of class? The chapters on writing and using objectives and on lesson planning will show you how to ensure the applicability and relevance of a lesson to adult learners' needs.

Be a Group Member Yourself

Become a real part of the learning endeavor by being a supportive, helpful, and friendly member of the group. Suppose you are enrolled in a class taught by a distant and cold instructor who has erected a barrier between teacher and student, a complete physical and psychological separation that no one is allowed to cross. You would probably soon become uneasy and unsure of yourself and unable to approach the teacher for help. This instructor is certainly not a member of the group seeking mutual answers to important questions. How do you feel? The chapters on adult learning and classroom management will discuss this concept and give you the insights into making group dynamics work for you.

Reinforce Learning Through Evaluation

Help yourself by helping your learners evaluate their own gains through feedback about their progress toward goals. Suppose you are a learner in a class where you never know where you stand. Your contributions to class discussion evoke no response. Assignments are graded without any formal or informal comments. You are not sure whether or not you are making any progress toward the goals you had for taking the class. You really don't know where or why you are not measuring up. How do you like it? The chapters on instructional objectives and evaluation will discuss how to use learner self-evaluation to help your learners understand both their progress and their problems, and help you assess your overall instructional efforts.

Develop a Collaborative Climate

Try to create a mutually respectful environment that is cooperative and relaxed, in which communication is shared openly. Suppose you are a learner in a class where it is perilous to speak. Your instructor is frequently dismissive or sarcastic and promotes learner insecurity. You and other learners are soon afraid to answer questions or get involved in hands-on exercises for fear of ridicule. The atmosphere is cold and unpleasant; the learners are resentful and suspicious. How do you respond? The chapter on classroom management will deal with this in greater detail.

Of course, you did not like any of the above scenarios. In the previous ten situations, you, as a learner, were being treated shabbily. While it is sometimes difficult to follow these ten recommendations for teaching adults all the time, you, as an instructor, can do your utmost to implement their substance and spirit. It is always helpful to put yourself in the learner's place as you instruct and use your own reaction as a guide.

Summary

This chapter has examined some very important instructor qualities, characteristics, roles and responsibilities, and basic instructional principles. In order to be as effective as possible, you must reflect on this information, making it a part of your belief system and putting it into practice through your actions. Doing so will ensure a high degree of professionalism and excellence in the classroom. The underlying theme of this book is the golden rule of adult instruction: *"Teach unto others as you would have others teach unto you."*

Chapter References

American Society for Training and Development. (1983). *Models for excellence: The conclusions and recommendations of the ASTD training and development competency study.* Washington, DC: Author.

GPU Nuclear Corp. (1986). *Training for performance: Basic instructor course text.* Parsippany, NJ: Educational Development Section; Training and Education Department, unpublished.

King, S.B., King, M., & Rothwell, W.J. (2001). *The complete guide to training delivery: A competency-based approach.* New York, NY: American Management Association.

Knowles, M. S. (1984). *Andragogy in action.* San Francisco: Jossey-Bass.

Kuchinke, K, & Peter, K. (eds.). (2000, March). *Academy of Human Resource Development, Conference Proceedings.* Raleigh-Durham, NC.

National Fire Academy (undated). Module #5: Teach others as you would have others teach unto you. In *Student manual: Principles of instruction.* Emmitsburg, MD: Author, unpublished.

National Fire Academy. (1989). *Fire service instructional methodology.* Emmitsburg, MD: Author, unpublished.

Robbins, D. M. (1990, October). Trainees know about training trainers. *Training & Development Journal,* 12-13.

Rosenbaum, B. L., & Baker, B. (1989). The trainer as a behavior model. In *Adult learning in your classroom* (pp. 7-8). Minneapolis, MN: Lakeland Books.

United States Army Corps of Engineers. (1982). *Instructional methods.* Washington, DC: Author, unpublished.

United States Department of the Navy. (1976). *Training specifications manual (Naval Air Maintenance Training Group).* Washington, DC: Author

2

Communication and the Instructor

Encourage active participation and three-way communication.

Well-developed communication skills are essential tools for instructors. It is through the communication process that your learners will learn from you, well as from each other—a three-way communication process. The purpose of this chapter is to provide you with the information necessary to develop effective instructional communication skills, such as speaking, listening, and questioning.

What is Communication?

Communication is defined as an imparting or conveying of knowledge or information from a source to a receiver (Anderson, 1988). It is a mutual exchange of facts, thoughts, opinions, and/or emotions. Unless information is both presented *and* received, communication cannot take place. The "circuit" must be complete.

You have probably heard (or maybe even said!): "That instructor knows the material, but sure can't get it across!" The inability to "get it across" means that an instructor has failed to communicate. To be an effective instructor you must develop the ability to express your ideas clearly and concisely—an essential instructional skill and tool. In your role as a behavior model and change agent, effective communication skills are crucial to the accomplishment of your training mission.

Instructional Communication

How does communication work? In the communication process, the sender creates a message that is conveyed (transmitted) to the receiver. Transmission is the point at which—and the method by which—the message is conveyed. The receiver takes in the message through one or more of the five human senses to form a mental perception and understanding of the message. Next, feedback, that is, a response from the receiver back to the sender, occurs. This is an important part of instructional communication: through this mechanism, the message is either clarified or a disparity in understanding is uncovered. The transfer of learning begins here.

In the classroom, your learner will be a sender as well as a receiver; this is especially true in adult education classes. Common classroom transmission devices include: voice, body language, video monitors, overhead projectors, pictures, tape recorders, and powerpoint presentations.

Of the three basic types of communication, *verbal, nonverbal, and paraverbal*, verbal communication refers to the spoken word. In the classroom, words may convey information, explanation, clarification, warmth, humor, etc. To use verbal communication effectively, keep your messages simple and easy to understand, and use many examples to illustrate your points. Keep the lines of communication open and working in both directions. Show and use your own personality to best advantage. Also, vary your voice in pitch, loudness, speed, etc., and use pauses and silence for effect.

It is true that actions speak louder than words: 55 to 65 percent of communication is transmitted nonverbally. Nonverbal communication refers to body language or the messages you send through facial expressions, gestures, posture, movements, etc. You must be able to use nonverbal communication effectively (see Kinetics Dictionary in the Appendix). Show your enthusiasm on your face: smile, nod, and make eye contact—be genuine. When communicating with your learners, be sure to respond to a raised hand and listen intently. Finally, the third form, paraverbal communication, refers to the way you make words sound—angry, happy, determined, sad, etc. The tone of your voice, movements of your body, etc., will sometimes speak louder than your words.

A Model of Verbal Communication

To best understand how communication works, a model, a simplified schematic of the communication process, is presented (Seiler, Schuelke, & Lieb-Brilhart, 1984). This communication model has seven components: (1) source, (2) message, (3) channel, (4) receiver, (5) environment, (6) feedback, and (7) noise. These interactive parts are illustrated in Figure 2-1. Since we are considering verbal communication, the model depicts an ear as the channel that receives sound waves. Other forms of communication (seeing, smelling, touching, and tasting) use other channels, such as the eye, nose, etc.

The source (sender) creates the message. When you, as the instructor are the source, the sound of your talking travels to your learners. A learner, when talking, becomes the source. Your job as an instructor (source) is to determine what is to be taught (communicated), and to try to put it (the message) into words (encode it), so that your learner (receiver) can understand (decode) it.

The receiver listens to the message and attempts to decode it. Successful interpretation allows the listener to store and recall the message and send feedback to the talker.

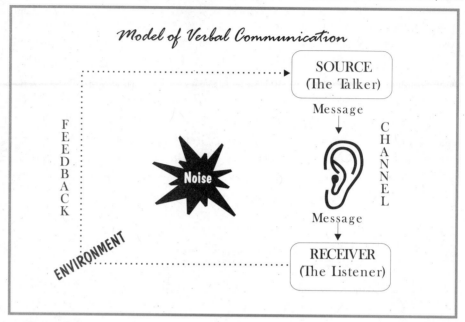

Figure 2-1.

The environment refers to the distance between the people involved, the atmosphere (attitudes, classroom, climate), and any other factors surrounding the talker and the listener. Communication can be ineffectual due to negative environmental factors, such as loud talking outside the classroom.

The feedback loop of the communication process lets the talker monitor the listener's response to the message. Feedback helps ensure that the exchange is accurate; it indicates whether or not communication has occurred between the sender and receiver.

Barriers to Communication

The communication model demonstrates a completed communication process from sender to receiver and back to sender. The model also shows that interference can and does occur throughout the process. This interference is called "noise" and affects any or all phases of the communication process. Noise can come from within the communication loop or from outside. Examples of such noise are actual noises in the area (cars, train whistle, TV, radio, someone else talking, etc.) or the thoughts (preoccupations) of either the sender or the receiver.

Removing barriers to communication plays an important role in determining whether communication will be successful. Communication is a multifaceted phenomenon. Simplistically, it can be considered only in terms of the sending and receiving of messages; however, the mere sending of the message does not ensure that the message has been received and, therefore, that a transaction has occurred. Even what seems to the talker (source) to be the simplest of messages can be misinterpreted by the listener (receiver). Often the message is only partially received or aborted entirely. The causes of partial or aborted messages can be environmental, emotional, due to inadequate verbal skill, or many other conditions that, collectively, are called barriers. In the instructional process, three basic problems can impede communications (Anderson, 1988, and furthered by Nihei, 2002): lack of a common core of experience, confusion between the symbol and the thing being symbolized, and overuse of abstractions.

Lack of a Common Core of Experience

Probably the greatest single barrier to effective communication is the lack of a common core of experience between communicator and receptor. Communication can be effective only to the extent that the physical, mental, or emotional experiences of the people concerned are similar or sufficiently explained. In the chapter on lesson planning (Chapter 6), I will describe methods to ensure that you and the learner begin instruction with a common basis for understanding.

Confusion Between the Symbol and the Thing Being Symbolized

Words are simply representations. They represent or correspond to anything that exists, is experienced, or is talked about. At best, language serves as a useful map, accurately representing a specified territory. Language should correspond to the objects or concepts that it represents. Like a map that contains errors, a statement that contains inaccuracies implies a relationship that does not exist.

Overuse of Abstractions

Concrete words (table, chair, car, etc.) refer to physical objects that human beings can experience directly. Abstract words, on the other hand, stand for ideas that cannot be experienced through the physical senses (hate, happiness, force). Abstractions cannot create mental images in the minds of the receivers. Abstract words are necessary and useful. Their purpose is not to bring forth specific items of experience in the minds of receivers, but to serve as shorthand symbols that sum up vast areas of experience.

Although abstractions are convenient and useful, their use can lead to misunderstanding. The danger in using them is that they will not produce in a listener's mind the specific items of experience that you as the speaker intend. The receiver has no way of knowing what experiences you intend an abstraction to include.

Planning for Effective Instructional Communication

Preplanning is essential and should be carried out at every stage of the instructional process, from knowing your audience to establishing the instructional objectives, from preparing the lesson plan and assembling materials and media to planning for an appropriate room or training facility. Planning is essential if you are to encourage active participation and three-way communication among you the instructor, the learner, and the class (Brookfield, 1986). A basic planning strategy is offered here and discussed in detail in Chapter 6 on lesson planning.

"First, tell them what you're going to tell them, next, tell them, and then tell them what you told them." This three-part model for speech-giving applies to lesson plans as well. Like a speech, a lesson plan contains an introduction (motivation/opening), a body (presentation/ application), and a conclusion (evaluation/ summary).

The *motivation/opening* should arouse the interest of your learners in the subject matter and intrigue them enough to want to learn more. It should also contain an overview of what learners can expect to learn from the lesson. The motivation/opening, therefore, should be designed to arouse interest and attention, promote friendliness and respect, and set the stage for the topics to be covered.

In the *presentation/application* section of your lesson plan, specific information and concepts (or skills) are presented, and learners may have a chance to apply what they have learned. To be most effective, the content should be arranged in a logical fashion. Some useful and logical methods for organizing content include chronological/sequential, comparative, procedural, problem/solution, categorical, cause and effect, or any other sensible patterning of ideas.

The *conclusion/evaluation* step of a lesson plan contains a testing mechanism to ensure that learning has taken place. At this point, too, the lesson is summarized and ending remarks are made. Useful conclusion/evaluation techniques include summarizing or restating material covered, enumerating key points, making an appeal or call for action (challenge), posing a rhetorical question, or making a prophecy. You can also conclude with certain devices often used in the motivation/opening step, e.g. a humorous story, a quotation, a compliment, a personal reference, or an illustration.

Speaking, listening, and questioning skills are the next areas of instructional communication which you will need to master in order to carry out an effective instructional presentation.

Speaking Skills

A basic principle of effective instruction is the concept of "easy talk," a technique taught at the National Fire Academy. This involves using clear and simple language when explaining something. Again, remember that words are only symbols for reality. When choosing the exact words to convey your message, use ones that best express the meaning you have in mind. Your words should have the same meaning for the listener as they do for you. Be specific to avoid misinterpretation. Where necessary, clearly define what you mean to avoid any possible confusion. Often I find that when some people assume an instructor's role, they suddenly talk in ways they never do in casual conversation with friends. They sometimes start talking in their "chief officer's" voice. They tend to forget the "keep it simple" rule and begin to insert a lot of unnecessary verbiage. They find it impossible to be natural. Being natural in front of a group is not easy—it takes practice. However, there are some things that you can try.

Use Words of High Frequency in the English Language (those often used)

Research indicates that when high frequency words are used, learning is faster and retention is longer. Using easy words and simple sentences in your writing and teaching is consistent with adult learning principles.

Use the Language of the Group

You should be flexible and skillful enough to adapt your language to the specific technical, intellectual, and age levels of the group. Talk to *express*, not to *impress*. Avoid controversial topics or language patterns (slang or off-color words) that may offend some class members. When you use language appropriate for your group, they will understand and you will establish rapport.

Use Terminology Familiar to the Subject or Group

Define any new technical terms as needed. This is especially necessary in technical subjects with very specialized terminology. Remember, it is better to oversimplify than risk misunderstanding or confusion. If either occurs, learners will tune you out. Certainly, difficult technical terms sometimes must be used. But the outstanding instructor can use simple words and illustrations to explain even difficult concepts.

Use Short Sentences

Generally, the shorter the sentence, the clearer the meaning. In addition, short sentences help the learners to pay attention. A long, wordy sentence may be confusing or tiring. Learners may forget what was said in the first part of the sentence. Precise, direct words put together in a clear, accurate, and logical manner make the best sentences. By using an easy conversational approach in leading a class, you will encourage others (your learners) to talk with you and with each other. Do not let your desire to communicate in an accessible fashion, however, cause you to slip into disrespectful, vulgar, or sarcastic verbal behavior. In addition, avoid a common barrier to learning—one-way communication (no feedback or learner-class loops). Each of us has experienced the drudgery of a class in which the instructor, like a rifle, fires information at us via one-way communication.

Clear explanations in guided learning and concise problem-posing in discovery learning create messages that can be decoded easily by the learners, which is essential for learning and memory. Again, keeping things clear invites rejoinder and casual conversation, which eliminates that destructive one-way communication. Words and sentences that convey exact information minimize misunderstanding or misinterpretation. For example, "Friday, the 5th of June, at 3:00 p.m." is much more specific than "a while ago." Individuals may interpret the time period of "a while ago" as an hour, yesterday, several months, or even several years, depending on their particular frame of reference.

Sharpening Your Platform Skills

Effective lecture presentations can be achieved through practicing certain platform skills. The following guidelines will help you instruct more successfully.

Your Voice

Speak in a natural, conversational manner—do not preach. Your tone of voice should be friendly and sincere. Be conversationally direct as if you were speaking with one individual. Avoid speaking down to the group in a haughty, indifferent, or impersonal manner. Speak to be understood. It is essential that you speak audibly and clearly, so that all participants can hear. Strive for clear projection—not too soft, not too loud. Your enunciation should be distinct and your pronunciation should be correct. Do not slur your words or mumble, and avoid or minimize verbal interruptions such as "uh," "er," "um," "all right," "okay," or the ubiquitous "you know." Never have objects in your mouth (e.g. gum, candy, etc.). Your rate of speech should be neither too slow nor too fast. Do not speak so slowly and distinctly that your presentation is unnatural. But, above all, avoid being so rapid that your audience is unable to follow you, a common fault of beginning or nervous speakers. Be sure to vary your pace to create interest. And avoid a deadly monotone by varying pitch, rate, and emphasis. Brief silences can be effective. You do not need to talk constantly. Always keep a glass of water or cup of coffee close at hand in order to avoid the dry throat syndrome.

Your Face

Move your head and make eye contact with the audience. Make each person feel that you are speaking to him or her. Avoid staring at one person. Look friendly, interested, and confident.

Your Body

If you are standing, move around and do not become frozen to the podium. Slight movements will loosen you up and allow for more eye movement on the part of the audience (avoiding eye fatigue). Maintain good posture. Be relaxed, but do not slump. Stand straight, but not rigidly. Use appropriate gestures (do not exaggerate) to accentuate major points. Occasional hands in pockets are natural, but do not keep your hands in your pockets too long—it may look awkward. Avoid fidgeting with objects in your pockets or in your hands—keys, change, markers, and pointers. Try to eliminate distracting mannerisms such as adjusting glasses, pacing, rocking from heel to toe, or swinging a foot.

The Podium/Table

Avoid clinging to, slumping over, or gripping the podium. If the podium is too big (or you are short), stand at the side or do not use it. If it is a distraction, remove it. Do not rap your fingers or tap your hands on the surface of the podium or table. This is particularly distracting when there is a microphone that magnifies every sound.

Public Speaking Anxiety

Public speaking often is frightening for a new instructor. After all, speaking in front of a group of strangers is not something you do every day. Take comfort in the fact that you are not alone in this fear. All new instructors experience much the same anxiety as you do.

How can we alleviate, or at least control, our anxieties? First, plan for your presentation. Using the information presented in this chapter and throughout the book will provide you with a base from which to plan and develop a sound lesson presentation. Next, practice your presentation once or twice—in front of a colleague or even in the privacy of your office in front of a mirror or on a tape recorder. If possible, get feedback to help you improve the presentation. These practice sessions will serve to make you more comfortable with the subject material. In addition, research your audience and know as much about them as possible.

Use supportive media such as projection transparencies, slides, or other graphics. As well as aiding you in presentation of the material, these media will give you something concrete to do and take the focus off you.

Be yourself—this is perhaps the most important suggestion I can give you. And remember, the more you speak in front of a group, the easier it will get.

Listening Skills

Effective listening is as important as effective speaking and is an integral part of nonverbal communication. Listening allows learners to absorb information, think, and learn. When listening, especially as an instructor, try to focus on understanding what is being said rather than getting ready to reply, contradict, or refute. Do not prepare your answer while listening, but rather be interested and alert, and do not interrupt. You should provide feedback, but avoid a negative response. Finally, remember that different learners will have varying abilities, language skills, and ways of expressing themselves—do not jump ahead of your learners, but let them go at their own pace. (Nihei, 2002, further highlights these points.)

Here are a few suggestions on how to use good listening skills to communicate effectively as an instructor. Successful lessons capitalize on the group's interactions with each other as well as with you, the instructor. Therefore, incorporate the following ideas into your repertoire of skills.

Send Positive Nonverbal Signals

Supportive, interested facial expressions, smiles, nods, etc. will convey to learners that you are listening to what they have to say. Maintaining good eye contact is another strong sign of interest (Hunter et al., 2005).

Use Encouraging Verbal Signals

Show interest in what the learner says and express a desire to know more of what they think by making short encouraging remarks, such as "Uh huh"; "Tell me more"; "What else?"; "Then, what?"

Restate and Repeat the Ideas or Context

Restatement can serve several purposes. It promotes understanding and acts as an accuracy check. It allows the speaker to hear his or her ideas expressed again so that he or she can amend or correct or expand what was said. It also shows the speaker that you have listened carefully and fully grasped what he or she has stated.

Allow for Learner Reflections

Listening carefully to learners encourages them to speak freely, with positive consequences for you, as well as them. You will be able to check on whether or not your learners have understood your instruction. They will be encouraged to continue and further elaborate, analyze, and clarify their thoughts. They will provide you with feedback and reaction that will assist you in recognizing, understanding, and accepting their feelings. And each time a learner speaks and reacts in class, others are encouraged to follow suit.

Use Questions Wisely

Open-ended questions encourage speakers to talk about their ideas or feelings and therefore do not limit the responses. Probes, used with sensitivity, can elicit more information and encourage your listener to think. Closed, or factual questions, often limit response and cut the speaker off.

Capitalize Upon Silence

Pauses need not be embarrassing. By not filling the vacuum, you let the speaker know that you are interested in what is being said and expect a further response. Silence can be used to organize one's own thoughts.

Remember to Summarize

During and at the end of a conversation or discussion, a summary of what has been said can clarify attitudes and reinforce understanding. It also conveys a sense of closure to the session.

Questioning Skills

Effective questioning is a key instructional skill. Questions are used in training for a variety of reasons, such as arousing curiosity and interest, stimulating discussion, channeling thinking, assisting in determining how well your learners understand the material, and encouraging your timid learners to express themselves.

Types of Questions

There are several types of questions. *Direct questions* are addressed to one specific person, giving that learner the opportunity to reply with specific information. *Overhead questions* are addressed to the entire group and are useful in promoting thinking, starting discussion, and eliciting different opinions. Anyone in the group or class may respond to an overhead question, but if no one reacts, such an inquiry easily can be converted into a direct question. And *rhetorical* questions are also addressed to the entire group; these are used to promote thinking and set a general theme. Such questions are not intended to produce an oral response. Upon receiving a question from a learner, you can turn it into a *relay question* by posing it to another learner. Relay questions can often result in valuable information conveyed from learners.

To be effective, all questions posed, regardless of type, should be brief, easily understood, and non-antagonistic. Ask questions in a friendly, sincere manner. Avoid asking questions that your learners cannot answer or that are too easy. Avoid asking questions that require simple "yes" or "no," or one-word responses. For example:

- *Poor question:* When the meter reads "0," do the circuits automatically close?
- *Better question:* What happens to the circuits when the meter reads "0"?

Actively Seek Feedback

In addition to such formal feedback methods as tests and quizzes, as an instructor you must question your learners constantly in order to achieve your instructional goals. Furthermore, a climate must be established in which the learners feel free to inquire. An instructor and an adult learner equally share the responsibility for ensuring that effective communication has occurred.

To keep your finger on the pulse of learner progress, you should use the following technique: ask a question, pause briefly, and call on one individual.

The best questions are those that ensure that both communication and understanding have occurred. These questions will elicit a brief explanation ultimately leading to a correct answer. You should involve all learners in your questioning; do not allow a few to monopolize the conversation. Also ensure three-way communication by allowing learners to answer each other's questions and concerns. By continuously maintaining a warm, open atmosphere of mutual respect and joint inquiry, the classroom climate will encourage feedback. Remember that feedback, either oral or written, is the only way to ever know if you have communicated successfully. Never just say, "Are there any questions?" Always ask specific questions requesting feedback (one point at a time) on material covered in the lesson.

Handling Responses

How you handle the responses to your questions is just as important as how you ask the questions themselves. If responses are not handled effectively, you risk alienating a learner—or even the whole class. To avoid this, promptly acknowledge correct replies. Give learners time to rephrase unclear statements. When your learners answer incorrectly, it is your responsibility to lead them to discover the correct response. If an incorrect answer is given, never ridicule, humiliate, or make the learner appear foolish to the rest of the class. Simply thank the individual and ask, "Are there any other opinions on this?"

When your learners ask you a question, give some thought to your response before making it. Or you can ask other learners to handle some of the response; this relieves you from being the sole respondent. For example, in response to a learner's inquiry, you might say: "Is there anyone else who has some insight into that?" or "What does someone else think?" Then, give your response after the class members have had their chance. If you do not know the answer, be honest. Tell your learners that you need to discover the answer to the question and will get back to them later with the information. Finally—and most significantly—try to be patient.

An Ultimate Communication Goal: Interaction Between Instructor and Learners

We, as instructors, must communicate on both the *content* and the *process* levels. Successful interaction between you and your learners requires careful attention to these two levels of communication. Content refers to the specific information or task upon which the class session will focus. It is concerned with the knowledge or skill to be learned. In order to be a credible and able instructor, you must be technically proficient (i.e. must know how to operate any equipment and perform all required skills). This is one half of the instructional process for which we are paid. However, only knowing the information does not qualify you to teach it. If you cannot "get the information across," then you have failed as an instructor.

The other half of our instructional expertise is process. This includes all other aspects of the instructional environment. It refers to the way the content will be communicated. It is also concerned with the relationship and/or rapport between learner and instructor.

A few suggestions for improving instructor/learner interaction follow below.

Create a Learning Climate

Communicate in ways that contribute to a positive learning climate for the group and demonstrate a positive model of behavior. Support people who try out new skills and experiences. Silber (2002) suggests a "cognitive approach that improves a learner's ulitmate problem-solving skills." Provide feedback that is descriptive and not evaluative. If the group flounders and becomes distracted from the overall purpose of the session, use techniques or exercises (verbal, nonverbal, etc.) to bring the group back on task.

Uphold your learning standards, even when the group does not follow them. When someone becomes critical or ignores the feelings of other people, articulate what you see happening to the group. Explain your concern about its effect on the group's learning climate.

Give Your Opinions and Express Your Feelings

Be a person. Be genuine. Let the learners realize that you too are part of the learning experience and a member of the group, and that you care about their concerns and problems. Use three-way communication.

Flow With the Group

Provide as many opportunities as you can for learners to experience success in identifying, analyzing, and generalizing. These experiences can be used to improve instructional skills and increase job performance.

See Yourself as a Resource Person

Be a helper/instructor in addition to the leader or key person in the group. Your learners have to go back to their jobs and be able to function without you. If you become too important, you will create dependency, and your learners will not be able to apply independently what they learned. So do not comment excessively or direct the group too often or speak before other group members can collect their thoughts. (McClure et al., 2003, adds contemporary thought concerning student-centered learning envionments.)

Respond to Situations as They Arise

Your feelings are your best guide. Trust your own ideas and do what seems right to you at the time. Later, reassess the situation and determine what you could have done differently. You are a learner, too. Effective interaction occurs, in essence, in a learning environment free from fear and intimidation. The creation of a supportive climate of mutual trust is your ultimate goal.

Summary

While the content of training may be predetermined, the way in which the learning takes place is flexible. The overall process is your professional responsibility. The choices made at this point grow out of your sensitivity toward your learners. When the concepts and suggestions described in this chapter and all others are considered, the process chosen will be learner-centered. Then learning will occur in the most effective manner possible.

To improve communication, review the effectiveness of your instruction at the end of each class session. Question yourself about both the instructional content and the process. (This is part of the post-course evaluation suggested in Chapter 9.)

- Do I understand that good teaching is good communication, and that it does not occur by chance alone?

- When I am thinking ahead about what I shall teach, do I put myself in the place of learners? Do I build my presentation around their skills and knowledge? Do I draw on what they already know?

- Is there a better way to handle what I have to say? Have I discovered a way to teach this content that is better than the way I was originally taught?

- What methods did I use in teaching today's material? Was my approach instructor-centered, learner-centered, or both? Are there alternative approaches?

- What did I do in my class to facilitate learning? To hinder learning?

- How much control did I exhibit today? How much flexibility did I allow? Was I "sticking to the lesson plan" at the expense of encouraging real learning to take place?

- What kind of impression did I create in the minds of my learners? Did they feel free to ask a question, comment on my presentation, or make mistakes?

- How did I handle questions asked by learners? Was I put off by the interruptions or did I try to use the questions to help the learners learn? Did I ask if there was anyone in the class who could answer, or was I only interested in demonstrating my own level of expertise?

If you honestly and openly answer the above questions in a process of self-evaluation, then continued improvement will occur. Barriers to communication will fade and effective interactions will take place. To instruct well means to communicate well. Effective communication is the lifeblood of every instructional setting.

Chapter References

Anderson, J. A. (1988). *Communication textbook.* Beverly Hills, CA: Sage, 1-150.

Brookfield, S. D. (1986). *Understanding and facilitating adult learning.* San Francisco, CA: Jossey-Bass.

Emergency Management Institute (EMI) (1987a). Discovery and clarity. In EMI, *Methods and techniques of adult learning.* Emmitsburg, MD: Author.

Emergency Management Institute (EMI) (1987b). Discussion as a major presentation mode. In EMI, *Methods and techniques of adult learning.* Emmitsburg, MD: Author.

Hunter, D., Gambell, T., & Randhawa, B. (2005, November). Gender gaps in groups listening and speaking: Issues in social constructivist approaches to teaching and learning. *Educational Review 57* (3), 329-355.

McClure, R. Johnson, B., & Jackson, D. (2003). *Assessing the effectiveness of a student-centered college classroom.* ERIC Research Report (ED 477743).

National Fire Academy. (Undated). Module #17: Use easy talk. In *Student manual: Principles of instruction.* Emmitsburg, MD: Author, unpublished.

Nihei, K. (2002, March). *How to teach listening.* ERIC Classroom Guide Report (ED 475743).

Seiler, W. J., Schuelke, L. D., & Lieb-Brilhart, B. (1984). *Communication for the contemporary classroom.* New York: Holt, Rinehart, and Winston.

Silber, K. H. (2002, March). Using the cognitive approach to improve problem-solving training. *Performance Improvement 41* (3): 28-36.

3

The Adult Learning Process

Recognize that individual adult learning speeds are going to differ, but, that as a person, each individual has the same privileges and worth.

You need a fundamental understanding of cognitive processing in order to be an effective instructor. Additionally, to be able to successfully lead the adult learner to mastery of a subject, you must be familiar with the science of andragogy, or adult learning. Adults are not children, and, as such, different principles of learning and instruction apply. The concept of *dignity* is vital here. As an instructor, you must, at all cost, ensure the dignity of your adult learner. A guiding rule stated by Arnold Bennett that applies here is that: "Your mind is a sacred enclosure into which nothing...can enter except by your permission."

It is your responsibility as an effective instructor to recognize the unique abilities, needs, and learning styles of each of your learners and select the appropriate instructional methods that will ensure success for each of these learners. To best accomplish this very difficult task, you first must acquire knowledge of the adult as a learner and the critical elements and processes of adult learning.

Characteristics of Adult Learners

Part of being an effective instructor involves understanding how adults learn best. Compared to children and teens, adults have special attributes and requirements as learners. While you must

The Adult Learner

- needs respect
- is autonomous and self-directed
- is goal-oriented
- is relevancy-oriented
- is practical
- has accumulated personal life experiences

Figure 3-1.

be familiar with adult learning theory and its relationship to the delivery of instruction in order to select and design appropriate programs, you first must be aware of the following characteristics of adult learners (Figure 3-1) in order to understand and work with the learner.

- As do all learners, adults need to be shown *respect*. Acknowledge and appreciate the wealth of experiences adult participants bring to the classroom. Treat everyone as your equal in experience and knowledge, and create an atmosphere in which learners are free to voice their opinions in class.

- Adults are *autonomous* and *self-directed*. They need to be free to direct themselves. Specifically, you can solicit learners' input on what topics to cover and have them work on projects that reflect their interests. Always encourage learners to assume responsibility for their research, presentations, group leadership, etc. Be careful to act as a facilitator, guiding these learners to acquire their own knowledge, rather than solely as a teacher, supplying them with facts. It is your responsibility to involve adult learners actively as participants in the learning process.

- Adults are *goal-oriented*. When beginning a course, they usually know what target they want to reach. Therefore, they appreciate a training program that is well organized and well designed to enable them to achieve their ends. You must be sure to identify goals and objectives up front in order to establish expectancies. Show your learners how your course will help them reach their goals.

- Adult learners are *relevancy-oriented*. They need a reason to learn; learning must relate to their work setting or other life responsibilities to be of value to them. Remember, you should always identify instructional objectives for adult participants before instruction begins. Relate new theories and concepts to material, concepts, situations, or settings familiar to learners. Remind your learners of what they already know, as well as how and when this new information offered in your course will fit in.

- Adults are *practical* and will focus on those aspects of a lesson that will be useful to them in their work. They may not be interested in knowledge for its own sake. Therefore, you must say explicitly how the material you present will be useful to participants on the job.

- Adults have accumulated a base of *life experiences and knowledge* from their work activities, family life, personal hobbies and interests, and previous training and education. Be sure to recognize the value of experience in learning. Learners need to relate new learning to their own knowledge and experience base. To help them do so, draw out from learners any experiences and knowledge relevant to the topic. You can also address this need by letting your learners work on projects that best reflect their own interests.

Critical Elements of Adult Learning

There are four critical elements of learning that must be considered in planning learning activities to ensure that learners do, in fact, learn. These elements are *motivation, reinforcement, retention,* and *transfer.*

Motivating the Adult Learner

A learner must be motivated to learn before any learning will take place. Even the most accomplished instructor will fail with a learner who remains indifferent, reluctant, or resistant. If a learner does not see the need for the information offered (or has been offended or intimidated), all efforts to assist that learner will be in vain. You must establish a rapport with all learners and prepare them for learning—this is motivation. You, as instructor, can create a climate for learning, using techniques to gain, build, and hold the interest of your learners, and provide encouragement. We will discuss how to do this in more detail in a later chapter (8) on motivation. However, you should be aware of several basic factors, each of which to some degree serves as a source of motivation for adult learning.

- *External expectations:* Adults learn in order to comply with the instructions, expectations, or recommendations of someone with formal authority.

- *Professional advancement:* Adults learn to achieve higher status in a job, secure professional advancement, absorb new information relevant to their performance, and keep up with the competition.

- *Social welfare:* Adults seek learning to improve their ability to serve others, prepare for service to the community, and improve their ability to participate in community work.

- *Cognitive interest:* Adults learn for the sake of learning; they seek knowledge for its own sake and to satisfy an inquiring mind.

- *Social relationships:* Adult learners seek out schooling and learning environments, in part, to meet a need for personal associations and friendships.

- *Escape/Stimulation:* Adults learn to relieve boredom, provide a break in the routine of home or work, or provide a contrast to other aspects of their life.

Therefore, you can motivate learners through several mechanisms, as described below:

- Set a feeling or tone for the lesson. Quickly establish a friendly, open atmosphere that conveys to your learners you will help them learn.

- Promote social interaction through activities and group discussions in your classroom. Allow your learners to interact with each other as much as possible.

- Show learners where the course content will be applied in their working situations. Stress the practical applications of the material whenever possible.

- Set an appropriate level of expectation. Adjust the level of tension to meet the level of importance of the content. If the material has a high level of importance, set a higher level of tension/stress in the class. Adults learn best under low to moderate stress; if stress is too high, it becomes a barrier to learning.

- Set an appropriate level of difficulty. The degree of difficulty should be set high enough to challenge your learners, but not so high that they become frustrated by information overload. Plan instruction to ensure a learner's success.

- Learners need specific knowledge of the results of their learning—called feedback. Feedback must be specific, not general, in nature.

- Learners also must see a reward for learning. The reward does not necessarily have to be monetary, as in a salary increase, but may simply show the learner what specific benefits will be realized from learning the material. Learners must be interested in the subject, and interest is directly related to reward. Adults must see the benefit of learning in order to establish an interest in the subject.

Barriers to Learning

In order to be an effective instructor, you must be aware of certain barriers to learning which adults often face. First, unlike children and teenagers, adults have many responsibilities that create obstacles to participating fully in the learning process. Some of these barriers may be a lack of time and/or money, scheduling difficulties, arranging for childcare, or transportation problems. Other barriers result from insufficient confidence or interest or information about opportunities to learn. You need to be sensitive to these problems.

Second, motivational factors can sometimes create additional barriers. What motivates some adults can act as a barrier to others. Typical adult education situations include learners who are taking training, not because they want to, but because they are required to, or have been (or expect to be) promoted, are seeking job enrichment, need to maintain old skills or learn new ones, have to adapt to job changes, or need to learn something to comply with local directives. Although many are spurred on to learn by such pressures, others become resentful and resist learning.

It is clear that the best way to motivate adult learners is simply to *increase* the motivators and *decrease* the barriers. Know why your audience is there (the motivators), and uncover what is keeping them from learning (the barriers). Then you can plan your motivating strategy. For example, show learners that your training program can help them win upcoming promotions or help them qualify to operate new equipment, and clearly demonstrate the relationship between training and increased job efficiency.

Reinforcement of Learning

Related to motivation is the learner's need for reinforcement. Learners must receive some encouragement or reward if learning is to begin and continue during and after the training process. This reward need not be tangible. But learners need to experience a sense of progress or success, either from your comments or their own observations and self-evaluation. Most people have only a limited tolerance for failure, and, as a wise instructor, you will plan the early stages of the program to ensure a high probability of learner success. Nothing motivates further learning better than the realization that one is learning something—nothing succeeds like success. Let's take a closer look at the concept of reinforcement.

Positive Reinforcement

Positive reinforcement is the process of rewarding or encouraging behavior that moves in the direction of the desired result. When teaching learners new skills, positive reinforcement is most effective. It involves rewarding accomplishment by attention, praise, marks, etc.

Negative Reinforcement

Negative reinforcement is the process of correcting or changing behavior that does not move in the direction of the desired result. When teaching replacement skills or correcting misinformation, negative reinforcement is most effective. It is useful in trying to get your learners not to do something, to change behaviors. The aim of negative reinforcement is *extinction*. In other words, negative reinforcement is used until the "bad" behavior disappears, or becomes extinct.

When changing behaviors (old practices), apply both positive and negative reinforcement until extinction occurs.

Reinforcement should be incorporated into the teaching/learning process to ensure correct behaviors. Use it on a frequent and regular basis early in the process to encourage learning and retention. Then, taper off—use reinforcement only on an intermittent basis to maintain behaviors. Intermittent reinforcement places the learning on a maintenance schedule.

Feedback

For reinforcement to be effective, there must be feedback to convey to the learner the result(s) of the training. Feedback should flow both from you, the instructor, to the learner and from the learner to you. In this way, all participants in the learning activity are given an opportunity to confirm progress, discuss concerns, and have input into the process. Both positive and negative feedback will occur. Any negative feedback must be tactfully handled; create a climate in which it is "OK" to criticize constructively. But beware! Negative feedback should never be directed at an individual in front of peers. Such discussion should take place one-on-one in a private location. Periodic oral or written questions to the group will elicit needed feedback. For more complex problems, private counseling/coaching will be necessary.

Retention of Learned Information

To benefit from formal training, your learners must retain learned information. Your job is not finished until you have assisted learners to retain, as well as understand, the information as taught. In order to do so, learners must be able to see a meaning or purpose for that information. If what is taught has real interest, importance, or relevance to learners, they are more likely to remember it.

It is equally important to realize that as time passes, how much is retained will be directly affected by the degree of original learning. Simply stated, if learners did not learn the material well to start with, they will not retain it very well either.

In addition, retention is directly affected by the amount of practice carried out by a learner during the learning process. We tend to remember more effectively when we use what we have learned. Practice should be emphasized early in the process to obtain perfection. After correct (desired) performance is achieved, practice should be distributed or assigned on a periodic basis to maintain the desired performance. Distributed practice thus is similar in effect to intermittent reinforcement.

Transfer of Learning

The end result of training is transfer of learning—the ability to use the learned information in the real world. Learners must be able to take what they have learned and apply it in new situations. As with reinforcement, there are two types of transfer: positive and negative.

Positive transfer, like positive reinforcement, will occur when your learner uses the behavior taught in the course.

Negative transfer occurs when your learner does not do what you asked but nevertheless, by chance, achieves a positive (desired) outcome.

Transfer of learning is most likely to occur in the following situations:

- if your learners can associate the new information with something they already know (*association*) (see Figure 3-2);
- if the information is similar to materials your learners already know, i.e., if it can be fitted within a logical framework or pattern (*similarity*);
- if your learners' degree of original learning was high (*degree of original learning*); and,
- if the information learned contains elements that are extremely beneficial (*critical*) on the job (*critical attribute element*).

The Learning Process

Let us turn our attention to a theory of learning and cognition and examine the adult as a learner. Dr. Robert M. Gagné of Florida State University describes the conditions of learning in terms of varieties of learned capabilities (Driscoll, 1994; Gagné & Briggs, 1979; Gagné, Briggs & Wager, 1988), and within the context of his information-processing model (Figure 3-3) (Gagné, 1977).

Gagné considers the activities involved in the acquisition of knowledge and skills to be learned capabilities. (Examples of the acquisition of knowledge and skills would be learning to drive a car, understanding advanced principles and theories of

An Example of Transfer by Association

Tell learners that you are going to teach them a new math system that is easy to understand. Very briefly show them the "new" symbols, equate them to Arabic numerals, and then remove from sight.

⌋ = 1   ⌈ = 6

⌊ = 2   ⌉ = 7

⌊ = 3   ⊓ = 8

⌉ = 4   ⌈ = 9

⬚ = 5   △ = 0

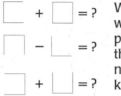

With no other explanation, have learners work the problems to the left. After they probably fail to get correct answers to all the problems, tell them that relating the new symbols to something already known will help them remember the new system.

Show the key element—the relationship of the symbols to that of a "tic-tac-toe" board. Numbering the board from left to right, beginning at the top, each symbol created by the segment of the "tic-tac-toe" board represents an Arabic numeral. The only truly new symbol to remember is that of a triangle representing the number "0." Now, learners should be able to solve the problems easily.

1	2	3
4	5	6
7	8	9

△ = 0

Therefore, when new information is related to something we already know, it becomes much easier to remember and is thus easier to transfer into use.

Figure 3-2. Source: National Fire Academy, 1989.

mathematics, appreciating the values of family life; etc.) These learned capabilities, he says, are internal (i.e., previously acquired) and are subject to external controls and manipulations (planned instruction). The categories of

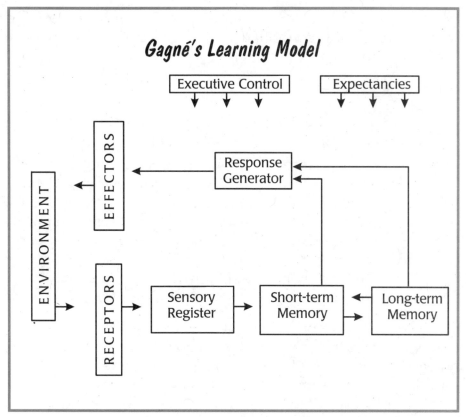

Figure 3-3. Source: R.M. Gagné and Driscoll, Marcy P. *Essentials of Learning for Instruction* (Needham Heights, MA: Allyn & Bacon, 1988). Reproduced with permission of Allyn & Bacon.

previously learned information and skills will be described later in the chapter.

Gagné's information-processing mode describes learning as information processing (Figure 3-3). In this model, stimulation received from the learner's environment (shown on left in Figure 3-3) activates the *receptors* and is transmitted as information to the central nervous system. This information (stimuli) is retained briefly in one of the *sensory registers* and is then transformed into recognizable patterns that enter into *short-term memory*. This transformation is termed *selective perception*. For instance, the visually presented marks on a page of print become letters such as *a, b, c,* etc., when stored in short-term memory. Most modern memory theory relies on analogies to computers to describe how we process information (e.g. working memory, buffers, encoding, retrieval).

Short-Term Memory

In the typical instructional process, information is received primarily through the senses of vision, hearing, and touch. This incoming information first resides in *short-term memory* (STM). But any information is stored there for only a very short time, usually less than 20 seconds, unless rehearsed. To illustrate this, a commonly used example is remembering a seven-digit telephone number. You can remember it just long enough to dial it. Once dialed, it disappears from short-term memory (STM), and, if needed for a longer period of time, must be rehearsed.

Short-term memory has a limited capacity as it can only hold a few separate bits of information at any one time. Some of that information is quickly forgotten from STM and never encoded into *long-term memory* (LTM). This limited storage capacity makes mastery of certain tasks much more difficult. For instance, one method of mentally multiplying 48×6 requires splitting the operations into two easier pieces. The intermediate operations (50×6; $300 - 12$) have to be held in STM. This requirement makes the accomplishment of such a task considerably more difficult than, say, 60×6.

Suppose that somebody read a list of 15 words to you at a rate of one every second (see Figure 3-4). After listening, you were asked to name all of the words you could remember. How many do you think you would be able to recall? You would actually be able to remember between 5 and 9 words. A characteristic of STM is that it can handle only between five and nine chunks of information at a time. Normal human capacity in STM is seven plus or minus two chunks of information (Miller, 1956). A chunk can be a word or a digit.

Example of the First Characteristic of STM

Read the following list of words to a learner at a rate of one every second. Have your learner write as many as can be remembered in any order, on a separate piece of paper. Do not allow the list of words to be studied beforehand. Just have your learner listen as they are read. Again, between five and nine words will be recalled correctly.

clock	lump	ball
wallet	car	coffee
pen	turtle	key
book	river	tree
hat	can	hammer

Figure 3-4.

As there is often more input into working memory than your learner can handle, new items will displace old ones. Old items of information, thus, are lost, as we try to accommodate new ones. We cannot handle an unlimited number of items in STM or working memory at one time.

Another characteristic of STM is that the information will be forgotten within about half a minute if you do not use rehearsal to retain it there (Anderson & Craik, 1974; Walls et al., 1982) (see Figure 3-5). Did you ever look up a telephone number, walk to the phone, and find that you had forgotten it before you were able to dial? Most people repeat the digits several times to themselves to maintain the phone number in STM (e.g. "594-2639, 594-2639, 594-2639"). This act of repeating the chunks of information in STM is called maintenance rehearsal. Maintenance rehearsal not only helps keep the items from being lost from STM, but it also may contribute to transfer of the information from STM to long-term memory (LTM).

Example of the Second Characteristic of STM

Spell the nonsense words in the list at the bottom of the box. Letters of the first nonsense word should be read to learners at a rate of one per second. Then, to prevent rehearsal, have the learners count backward (aloud) from a number like 238 (237, 236, and so on) for 5 seconds until you say "write." Have the learners try to spell the nonsense word. Even without rehearsal, they probably will be able to spell the first word because only 5 seconds elapsed. For the second nonsense word, the procedure is repeated, but have them count backward for 10 seconds before saying "write." Many learners will still spell correctly because it usually takes about half a minute for information in STM to fade. However, when they are asked to spell the third nonsense word after a nonrehearsal period of 45 seconds, it is very unlikely that they will be able to do so. If they had been allowed to use maintenance rehearsal, the task would have been easy, because information can be maintained indefinitely in STM if it is constantly rehearsed.

B-W-T-L (5 seconds)

J-S-V-K (10 seconds)

H-R-N-P (40 seconds)

Figure 3-5.

Thus, research has identified two major characteristics of STM. First, the capacity of STM for most people is 7 plus or minus 2 chunks of information (i.e., 5, 6, 7, 8, or 9 chunks of data). Second, information in STM will be forgotten within about half a minute unless maintenance rehearsal is used. With maintenance rehearsal, information can be maintained in STM as long as desired. You should clearly understand that short-term memory is but one stage of the process of learning.

Long-Term Memory

Information, which is to be remembered or recalled repeatedly, is again transformed by a process called semantic encoding into a form that enters long-term memory (LTM). When encoded in this way, information in long-term memory becomes more meaningful and takes the form of language, possessing sentence-like subjects and predicates (Gagné & Briggs, 1979). In this form, information may be stored for long periods of time. It can then be retrieved to short-term memory as needed. It can be combined with other information to form new information (hence new kinds of learning). When these events take place, the memory is referred to as working memory.

The first characteristic of LTM is that information transferred from STM to storage in LTM is reorganized, if necessary, and is assimilated with existing knowledge (see Figure 3-6). Learners who cluster similar ideas together remember the material much

---

Example of the First Characteristic of LTM

Look at the list at the bottom of this box. Use 2 minutes (120 seconds) to tell a story to yourself linking the 10 words together in order. For instance, your story might start as follows: "The man stuck his *head* in the *stove* because he was drunk on *whiskey*. There was *butter* dripping out of his hip pocket when ..." Research indicates that the more bizarre your story is, the more likely you are to remember it (and the words in the correct order). After 2 minutes, try to tell yourself the story you made up and write the 10 words in order on a piece of paper. The fact that you probably remembered 9 or 10 words and probably will be able to recall them tomorrow is testimony that LTM involves assimilation (connection) of the new material to be learned (a list of words) to familiar cognitive structures (the structure of the story you make up).

| head, | stove, | whiskey, | butter, | thief, |
| door, | lion, | moon, | salt, | bed. |

Figure 3-6.

longer than those who do not cluster. Learners who use mnemonic devices (i.e., memory devices, discussed later in this chapter) to link new information to old remember the material much longer than those who do not use mnemonics. Learners who generate semantic meaning or elaborations of the material to be learned remember the material much longer than those who do not generate meanings and elaborations.

Referring back to the model, you should realize that information from either working memory or long-term memory is transformed into action when retrieved and passed into a response generator (Figure 3-3). A message activates the effectors (muscles), producing an observable performance in the learner. This is the action which enables an external observer, such as an instructor, to tell that the initial stimulation has had the expected or desired effect. Information has been processed and the learner has learned.

The second characteristic of LTM is that storage is relatively slow, but retrieval is fast. LTM has huge capacity for storage (see Figure 3-7). We are in no danger of filling it up. It appears to take about 5 seconds to transfer a chunk of information from STM to LTM.

Some current speculations about LTM are interesting, but have not yet been firmly established. Many researchers believe that once a chunk gets encoded in LTM, we never really forget it. We may think we have forgotten it, but it is only because we cannot find where it is stored in LTM, and so cannot retrieve it. For example, Wilder Penfield, a Canadian neurosurgeon, touched particular locations of the exposed brains of some patients under local anesthetic and caused them to remember long-forgotten events, songs, and information.

Information Processing Control

To understand Gagné's model (Figure 3-3), you must be familiar with two important structures: *expectancies* and

Example of the Second Characteristic of LTM

As another person (perhaps a learner) reads the list at the bottom of this box, see how fast you can think of the answers. If you know the answer at all, you can probably think of it in 1 second or less. When someone asks the name of the painting by Leonardo da Vinci which portrays a woman with an intriguing smile, you can probably respond, "the Mona Lisa," almost immediately. You might not have thought about it for years; yet, you can retrieve the fact, if it is in LTM, in a fraction of a second.

- ☐ Who is Superman's girlfriend?
- ☐ Who is Batman's sidekick?
- ☐ Who is Tarzan's wife?
- ☐ What was the name of Roy Rogers' horse?
- ☐ Who was the lead singer of The Beatles?
- ☐ Where was Napoleon defeated?

Figure 3-7.

executive control. These are the processes that activate and modulate the flow of information during learning. For example, when learners have an *expectancy* (an idea) of what the outcome of the instruction will be, this anticipation will influence how they perceive the external environment. Expectancies affect how new information is encoded into the learners' memory and how it is eventually transformed into performance. This is one reason why learning how to develop instructional objectives for our learners (Chapter 4) is of such importance.

The *executive control* structure governs the use of cognitive strategies, which may determine how information is encoded when it enters long-term memory, or how the process of retrieval is carried out. Mnemonic devices are one cognitive strategy adult learners often use. (I will discuss these devices in greater detail later in the chapter.) The model (Figure 3–3) introduces the structures underlying contemporary learning theory and indicates a number of processes. All of these processes comprise the events that occur in an act of learning. These are:

- reception of stimuli by receptors;
- registration of information by sensory registers;
- selective perception for storage in short-term memory;
- rehearsal to maintain information in STM;
- semantic encoding for storage in long-term memory;
- retrieval from LTM to working memory (STM);
- response generation to effectors;
- performance in the learner's environment; and,
- control of processes through executive strategies.

In order to be effective as an instructor, you must realize that external events can be manipulated to influence the processes of learning for a learner. The internal processes cited above can be enhanced by external events that take place in the learning environment. For instance, learning the parts of a clock can be aided by using a diagram. Semantic encoding of specific sentences in a book can be done more easily if these sentences are in bold letters.

Instruction and the Process of Learning

Your primary objective throughout the development of instruction will be to influence the internal events or processes of learning through manipulation of the external events. By altering the external events (of instruction), an instructor can affect these processes in a variety of ways, many of which are supportive of learning. I will describe many of these ways in future chapters. In essence, as Gagné, Briggs and Wager (1988) have often stated: "Instruction may be conceived as a deliberately arranged set of external events designed to support internal learning processes" (p. 11).

The following nine events of instruction are patterned after Gagné's model.

- Stimulate to *gain attention* to ensure the reception of stimuli.

- *Inform learners of the learning objective* to establish appropriate expectancies.

- *Remind learners of previously learned content* for retrieval from LTM into working memory.

- *Clearly and distinctively present material* to assure selective perception.

- *Guide learning* to ensure suitable semantic encoding.

- *Elicit performance* to involve response generation.

- *Assess the performance*, involving additional response feedback occasions.

- *Provide feedback* about performance.

- *Arrange for variety of practice* to aid future retrieval and transfer.

The Contribution of Memory

In addition to the external events of instruction, you should be aware of certain internal events of instruction that affect the conditions of learning. Gagné describes these as the presence in working memory of certain *memory contents*. Memory contents are retrieved from LTM during the learning episode when your learner is asked to recall previously gained information. The contents of LTM, when retrieved into working memory, become essential parts of the conditions of learning. The contents of memory can be differentiated into five general categories or classes.

- *Intellectual skills*—the discriminations, concepts, ideas, and higher-order principles which need to be recalled (via cues) to permit the learner to carry out symbolically controlled procedures such as identifying the hypotenuse of a triangle or selecting the correct verb for a sentence.

- *Cognitive strategies* for learning and remembering—the internal means by which learners exercise control over their own learning processes. These can include image links such as mnemonic devices.
- *Verbal (factual) information*—the facts and organized knowledge of the world stored in memory. Internally, these can, for example, include linguistic rules. Externally, knowledge of the objectives of instruction aids in verbal information recall.
- *Motor skills*—the movements of skeletal muscles engaged to accomplish purposeful actions.
- *Attitudes*—internal conditions that influence the personal action choices a learner makes.

You, as an effective instructor, must realize that instruction cannot concentrate solely on any one of these classes of learned capabilities. The human learner needs to use many kinds of learned capabilities in almost all learning situations.

A Word about Mnemonic Devices

Mnemonic devices are helping devices that can be used by your learner to associate the to-be-learned material with familiar information in LTM. Memory books and seminars on "How to Remember" often use mnemonics as the major vehicle. Nightclub and TV acts in which someone demonstrates "incredible" memory feats are built on mnemonics like Digit-Consonant-Encoding. This is a rather difficult device to acquire, but once mastered, it can produce dramatic results.

The usual purpose of a mnemonic device is to tie the material we are trying to learn and remember to something that is already familiar to us. It is a way of giving meaning to something that has little meaning to us when we begin to learn it. Later, when the material becomes a well-established part of our cognitive structure in LTM, the mnemonic can be discarded. Some, however, may persist throughout our lives. For example, many of us still use the rhyme to remember how many days are in each month: "Thirty days hath September, April, June, and November. All the rest have 31, except February, for which 28 is fine, until leap year comes along and makes it 29."

The research on mnemonics has yielded consistent findings. Almost any type of mnemonic will speed initial learning and aid long-term retention. As would be expected, some are more appropriate for one kind of material than for other kinds. In general, however, mnemonics are extremely effective for facilitating memory when they are used properly.

Use Mnemonic Devices to Aid Your Learner in Verbal Information Recall

Mnemonic or memory devices aid in building success chains and can be useful when integrated in your instruction. Some types of mnemonics are: Loci Mnemonics, Peg-Word Mnemonics, First-Letter Mnemonics, Rhyme Mnemonics, and Encoding Mnemonics (Bellezza, 1981). An example of each of these devices is provided below (Belleza, 1981; in NFA, undated, Module #14).

Loci Mnemonics

Many mnemonics require your learner to picture visual images. For example, when using a loci mnemonic, your learner mentally pictures the words to be learned in a series of locations (such as a walk through town). Research indicates that the more bizarre the images connecting a place and an item to be remembered are, the more easily they will be remembered.

Suppose that you had to remember (1) fuel oil, (2) turpentine, (3) acetylene, (4) olive oil, (5) gasoline, and (6) carbon monoxide in the order of their ignition temperatures. Imagining a walk through your house, you might visualize (1) a can of fuel oil as the doorknob to your front door. Behind the door is your umbrella stand on which someone has spilled paint and filled it with (2) turpentine. It is obvious that the person also tried to remove the paint with (3) an acetylene torch. This upsets you, so you go to the kitchen for a beer, but there is (4) olive oil all over the floor. You skid to the refrigerator, but when you open the door, you see 100 cans of (5) gasoline. To top it off, you notice that the name on the stove is no longer "General Electric," but (6) "Carbon Monoxide." These bizarre mental images may seem silly, but certainly can help learners remember a series in order by tying them to familiar locations (loci).

Peg-Word Mnemonics

Peg words are similar to loci in that they give the learner something (a peg) on which to hang the items to be learned. The peg words must first be memorized: 1 is bun, 2 is shoe, 3 is tree, 4 is door, 5 is hive, 6 is sticks, 7 is heaven, 8 is gate, 9 is wine, 10 is hen.

Now suppose that you wish to remember sawdust, paper, wood, gasoline, and asphalt in order. You might visualize: (1) a bun filled with sawdust; (2) a shoe with paper on the inside to cover the hole in the bottom; (3) a tree with some of the bark missing so that the wood shows; (4) a door that says "unleaded" covering a gasoline cap; and (5) a beehive made out of asphalt. Again, this use of peg words may seem bizarre, but research indicates their efficacy for LTM is overwhelming.

First-Letter Mnemonics

The first letter of the items to be remembered can often be arranged into a sentence or word. For example, "HOMES" can help you remember the five great lakes—Huron, Ontario, Michigan, Erie, and Superior.

Rhyme Mnemonics

In a rhyme mnemonic your learner uses a chain of linking information. In the case of a rhyme the items are forced into meter and rhyme to make them easier to recall. The example ("Thirty days hath September, April, June, and November...") is an excellent example of imposing rhyme structure on essentially unconnected material to improve memory.

Suppose we want an easy rhyme to remember the fire flow formula. "GPM (gallons per minute) is said to be, length times width divided by three. Multiply this by the number of floors, and you will know the total score." Such a jingle can make things easier to learn and remember.

Encoding Mnemonics

Numbers are often particularly hard to remember. A digit-consonant-encoding mnemonic can help. It is, however, a difficult technique to begin using. Nightclub and TV super memory acts that involve remembering many numbers are built around this system (although a larger version than the one described here). The digit-consonant pairs must first be mastered; then, they can be used to remember any number (e.g. telephone numbers). In the key sentence "SaTaN May ReLiSH CoFfee Pie," the consonants (or sounds) are learned with digits. The keys from this key sentence are S = 0, T or D = 1, N = 2, M = 3, R = 4, L = 5, SH or G = 6, C = 7, F = 8, and P = 9.

Suppose a person wanted to remember the phone number 546-4120. The phrase "LARGE RED NOSE" would do it. By referring to the keys, L = 5, R = 4, G = 6, R = 4, D = 1, N = 2, S = 0 (zero). Maybe one could visualize the person having that phone number as having a large red nose. Let's try another one; 291-3929 can be translated to NaP TiMe oN SHiP. As noted, digit-consonant encoding is difficult to use and should probably be attempted only by those willing to invest time and effort in improving memory skills.

Summary

You must remember that learning occurs within each individual, and is a continual process throughout everyone's life. We all learn at different speeds, and it is natural for us to be anxious or nervous when in a learning situation. Positive reinforcement can enhance learning, as can proper timing of the training.

In closing, recognize that individual adult learning speeds are going to differ, but, each individual has the same privileges and worth.

Chapter References

Anderson, C. M. B., & Craik, F. I. M. (1974). The effect of a concurrent task on recall from primary memory. *Journal of Verbal Learning and Verbal Behavior, 13,* 107-113.

Bellezza, F. S. (1981). Mnemonic devices: Classification, characteristics, and criteria. In National Fire Academy. (Undated). Module #14: *Never forget good old what's his name.* Emmitsburg, MD.

Driscoll, M. P. (1994). *Psychology of learning for instruction.* Needham Heights, MA: Allyn & Bacon.

Gagné, R. M. (1977). *The conditions of learning,* 3rd ed. New York: Holt, Rinehart and Winston.

Gagné, R. M., & Briggs, L. J. (1979). *Principles of instructional design,* 2nd ed. New York: Holt, Rinehart and Winston.

Gagné, R. M., Briggs, L. J., & Wager, W. W. (1988). *Principles of instructional design,* 3rd ed. New York: Holt, Rinehart and Winston.

Miller, G. A. (1956). The magical number seven plus or minus two: Some limits on our capacity for processing information. *Psychological Review, 63,* 81-97.

National Fire Academy. (1989). *Fire service instructional methodology.* Emmitsburg, MD: Author.

Walls, R. T., Haught, P. A., & Dowler D. L. (1982). *How to train new skills: Planning, teaching, evaluating.* Dunbar, WV: Research and Training Center Press.

4

Writing and Using Instructional Objectives

Help your learners set goals and understand why they need to learn a topic.

In order to be an effective instructor, you must continually monitor the proficiency of your instructional design and delivery. Instruction can be successful only to the degree that it instills the desired learner behaviors. And, in order to ensure effective instruction, a documented need for training must exist. When your learners do not use the subject matter taught on their jobs or if they already know what is being taught, instructional effort is wasted. Therefore, your first job is to determine what are the training needs of your firm or organization, and then develop instructional objectives to meet those needs.

Goals and Objectives

A *goal* is a general statement of the purpose or outcome of a lesson (Mager, 1984). It is not necessarily stated in terms of observable learner performances. However, an *instructional objective* is a precise statement of what your learner will be able to do at the end of the instruction, stated in behavioral terms (Mager, 1984; Cantor, 1986a; 1988). Heinich et al., (2002) further discusses instructional objectives.

Instructional objectives must be measurable, never vague. Since instructional objectives focus on observable performances, you must use "observable" verbs to describe

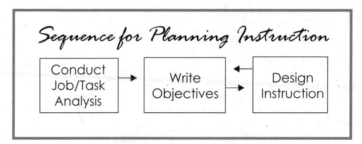

Figure 4-1.

what learners are to do (e.g. demonstrate, list, define) versus "nonobservable" ones (e.g. think, understand). Always remember that instructional objectives should focus on what learners will do, not on what you, the instructor, will teach.

Instructional objectives can form a bond of common understanding between you, as the instructor, and your learner. They provide a form of instructional communication. Furthermore, instructional objectives enable your learners to form *appropriate expectancies* about their new learning situation and establish useful internal conditions to ensure suitable *semantic encoding* of new information.

Before writing instructional objectives, a needs assessment should indicate that training is actually necessary (Cantor, 1986a; 1988). Only *after* this assessment clearly indicates the need for training and *before* the instruction is planned and designed, should instructional objectives be prepared. In addition, an occupational or job analysis must be conducted to detail the procedures for which formal training is required. This again always *precedes* the writing of instructional objectives. Figure 4-1 above illustrates this proper sequence.

The Importance of Instructional Objectives

An instructional objective is a statement of exactly who the learner is, what the learner must perform, under what circumstances or conditions, and to what degree or standard of proficiency. The best indication of a useful instructional objective is the learner's performance after instruction. If your learners perform in a manner that is consistent with the objective, then you have constructed a useful instructional objective.

Provide Communication

Instructional objectives provide the communication link between you, as the instructor, and your learners. And, good communication, through clear and concise instructional objectives, promotes better education. Both the instructor and learners know immediately what is expected of them and can determine what they must do to meet expectations, especially important in distance learning environments.

Demonstrate Quality

People other than learners may read your instructional objectives; for example, training and corporate management may wish to evaluate them. If your objectives are both useful and well written, these people can recognize more readily the quality and value of your training program.

Focus on the Need-to-Know

Well-designed instructional objectives will help you stay on track in your presentations. I often find that novice instructors tend to include too much material. You must be sure to identify and present only the information and skills necessary to facilitate your learners' attempts to meet the instructional objectives. Almost any text or other source material you select will contain some "extra" or "nice-to-know" information for which the learners should not be held accountable. By referring to sound instructional objectives when planning lesson content, you can avoid wandering too far from the purpose and becoming "material-oriented." You can then focus on the "need-to-know" information necessary to accomplish the job.

Aid in Methods/Media/Materials Selection

You first must know exactly *what* you are to teach in order to make intelligent decisions on *how* to teach it. Then, instruction is greatly enhanced by the selection of appropriate instructional methods, media, materials, etc. Well-defined instructional objectives will be invaluable in helping you choose the most appropriate ways to impart the required knowledge and skills to your learners (see Chapters 7 and 10).

Ensure Better Evaluation

The degree of success that learners exhibit in your class must be measured and recorded. As an instructor, evaluation of both your own instruction and your learners' mastery of the information and skills will be one of your major responsibilities. The only way that you and your learners can know if your training has been effective is when they can perform in the desired manner as outlined in the objective. Well-constructed instructional objectives are used as a standard—both for learner acquisition of skills and knowledge, and for training program evaluation (see Chapter 9). Evaluation instruments, such as tests, exams, verbal questions, etc., have to be constructed to measure what learners must master. If you base questions on the instructional objectives of the course, the test will reflect what must be mastered and thus be fair to learners. The tests also will be accurate in measuring the appropriate learner levels of performance (see Chapter 5).

Facilitate Learning

Perhaps the most important reason for planning and providing instructional objectives is to make the learning process easier for the learners. You may remember taking courses where clear-cut objectives were not supplied. In this situation, you probably spent too much of your time trying to figure out what you were supposed to learn. If clear-cut objectives had been supplied, you would have been able to master more useful information in a shorter period of time. There is no reason to keep instructional objectives hidden from the learners. Involve them in the course and let them be accountable for their own progress by telling them where they are headed (they can then *form appropriate expectancies*) and what is expected of them (to *maximize selective perception*). With clearly defined and well-written objectives, learners' efforts to learn are more efficient and therefore they can understand and retain (*selectively perceive*) more material in any given lesson or course. In addition, you will be more organized and effective if your teaching efforts are directed toward helping your learners achieve the lesson's instructional objectives.

After reading and practicing the ideas in this chapter, you will become proficient in recognizing well-written instructional objectives. You will learn how to classify, plan, and construct effective instructional objectives—ones that will provide guidance and direction for both you and your learners.

Needs Assessment

Needs assessment is a term used in business and industry to describe the process of determining if there is a need for specific training within an organization. You, as an instructor, should use the most appropriate and feasible methods possible to determine training needs. Methods may include talking with such knowledgeable people within the organization as job incumbents, supervisors, engineers, managers, etc., looking at records of errors made on the job, examining news reports, developing and administering a questionnaire, or consulting other sources of information. Training needs are identified by noting discrepancies or gaps between what *should be* happening on the job, and what *is actually* happening. Figure 4-2 presents a series of guiding questions to carry out a needs assessment for training (Cantor 1986b).

Once you have determined a need for training, you must identify what specific information must be taught. A very

Questions to Facilitate a Training Needs Assessment

☐ What is the discrepancy or gap between what is and what ought to be?

☐ Is the need (discrepancy or gap) documented anywhere (e.g. survey, task force report)?

☐ What are the consequences if the need is not met, and are these consequences documented anywhere?

☐ What caused the need (discrepancy or gap) to be brought to your attention at this particular time (e.g., new law, updated safety standards, pressure from public opinion, technological change, fiscal restraints, need for improved service)?

☐ Is it a training problem (couldn't do it if their lives depended on it), a motivation problem (*could* do if their lives depended on it), or a problem that changing something in the environment will fix?

Figure 4-2.

important rule in adult training and education, especially in business and industry, is to teach learners only what they need to know to perform a job properly. Subjecting them to a rehash of knowledge they have already mastered is insulting and boring. You must concentrate on teaching the learner to master the body of knowledge and/or skills necessary to meet the specific training needs (Cantor, 1986b; Cantor, 2000; Cross, 1981; Knowles, 1980).

Occupational Analysis

The next step, after deciding that a specific need for training exists, is to analyze that need in detail to determine which specific jobs and tasks are to be taught. This process is called an occupational and task analysis.

Occupational analysis is a broad term used to describe the systematic process of defining or describing an entire job or job category, e.g. that of a chemical technician. Often the training staff of an organization will be involved in performing this kind of analysis. More often, however, you will be required only to identify the training necessary at a more specific level within a job category; this process is usually referred to as job and task analysis, or task analysis, in its shorter form. The goal of task analysis is to achieve a better understanding of both the task and how those who will perform it should be trained and evaluated.

Task Analysis

Task analysis is the process of breaking down the task into functional behavioral units (Walls, Haught, & Dowler, 1982; Spaid, 1986). When conducting a task analysis, specify the exact behaviors your learner must exhibit to perform the task.

As described in various military and federal government models for instructional development, an entire occupational analysis can be thought of as a tree. The thick branches at the top are called *jobs*. Jobs are the major divisions within an occupational field. In law enforcement these jobs might be: (a) Crime Prevention, (b) Patrol, (c) Emergency Services, (d) Detection, and (e) Community Education.

The second level (thinner branches) is called *duties*. Duties are the logical subsets of jobs. These often comprise about the amount of material that would be covered in a single training lesson. For example, some units under "Patrol" might be: (a) Traffic Laws and Procedures, (b) Traffic Control, (c) Controlled Access Highway Patrol, and (d) Deploying Personnel and Equipment.

The third level (even thinner branches) is called *tasks*. Tasks are the logical subsets of duties. They are often approximately the size of a single instructional objective within a lesson. For example, some tasks under "Deploying Personnel and Equipment" in a Police Science Course might be: (a) Dispatch Unit, (b) Set Up Equipment, (c) Provide Backup, and (d) Provide Other Support Agents.

The fourth level (yet thinner branches) is called *task elements*. Task elements are the logical subsets of tasks. They are often about the size of a supporting or enabling instructional objective in a course. For example, some task elements under "Provide Backup" might be: (a) Select Backup Sources and (b) Establish Communications.

The fifth level (thinnest branches) is called *steps* (under task elements). Steps are the operations required to perform tasks or jobs. For example, some steps under "Establish Communications" might be: (a) Turn On 2-Way Radio, (b) Shift to Transmission Frequency, (c) Push Mike Button, (d) Speak Clearly, and so on.

It is sometimes difficult to determine how much detail should be used in breaking down the task. For example, would it be better to break the "Turn on 2-way radio" into two steps? (1) Grasp the switch with thumb and forefinger, (2) Move the switch to the ON position. Or would it be better to combine them into one set? (1) Throw the switch to the ON position. The answer is that it depends on your learners. The general recommendation is that learners with lesser prerequisite skills will need a more finely detailed analysis with more steps (smaller bites). When doing a task analysis, write steps of a size that seem reasonable to you. Then, if experience in teaching the task reveals that the task should be broken down into smaller steps, add more sub-steps to your task analysis. Thus, different task analyses written for the same task may include more or fewer steps, depending on the learning history of your learners. A sample job and task analysis is diagrammed in Figure 4-3. As a result of making such a detailed diagram, the identified training need is mapped, and instruction can now be designed. The figure shows where your learners' entry-level skills actually are and,

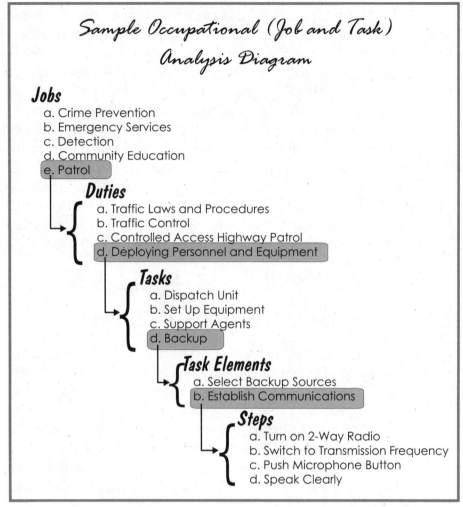

Sample Occupational (Job and Task) Analysis Diagram

Jobs
   a. Crime Prevention
   b. Emergency Services
   c. Detection
   d. Community Education
   e. Patrol

Duties
      a. Traffic Laws and Procedures
      b. Traffic Control
      c. Controlled Access Highway Patrol
      d. Deploying Personnel and Equipment

Tasks
         a. Dispatch Unit
         b. Set Up Equipment
         c. Support Agents
         d. Backup

Task Elements
            a. Select Backup Sources
            b. Establish Communications

Steps
               a. Turn on 2-Way Radio
               b. Switch to Transmission Frequency
               c. Push Microphone Button
               d. Speak Clearly

Figure 4-3.

accordingly, where training is needed and should begin (Dick & Carey, 1978).

A task analysis will also help you design a teaching strategy and diagnose any instructional problems encountered during or after instruction. I have found that it also helps to flowchart the tasks for competence in instructional preparation, lesson presentation, learner application, and finally, learner and lesson evaluation.

During lesson preparation, a good task analysis that helps you fully understand the task will help you decide the best method for instruction. For example, if a given task has multiple steps, you may decide that it would be inappropriate first to lecture on and then to demonstrate all of the steps in a single session. Instead, you may decide that a better plan would be to pause after teaching the first six steps and evaluate learner mastery to that point. In this way you can make sure that those six steps are mastered before going on to subsequent steps. Thus, task analysis can help you plan a reasonable approach that will result in quicker acquisition of skills by your learners and less frustration for you as well. A task analysis will also prove helpful later in learner and lesson or course evaluation (see Chapters 5 and 9).

Developing Instructional Objectives

Once the job and task analysis is completed, decisions about what information should be presented formally must be made. This will require answers to questions such as: What must your learner do immediately when beginning the job? What can your learner learn less formally on the job? What is critical to job performance regardless of when your learner will be called upon to perform the task? Once these kinds of questions are answered, you are ready to write your instructional objectives.

Format of an Instructional Objective

A well-written objective has a standard format. This format includes four parts: audience, behavior, condition, and degree (or standard) (National Fire Academy, 1989; Heinich et al., 2002, underscores this process). When writing an instructional objective, you must be sure that your learners (audience) know exactly what you want them to do (behavior), under what circumstances they will be asked to perform (condition), and how well they must perform (degree or standard). If you consciously include the audience, behavior, condition, and degree or standard in your objectives, you can be sure that learners and other instructors will find them clear and concise. Thus, when writing your instructional objective, you must make sure that the person reading the objective can readily answer four questions:

- Exactly who are the intended learners? (AUDIENCE)
- Exactly what do you want the learner to do? (BEHAVIOR)
- What conditions and/or limitations will the learner be operating under when they do what you want them to do? (CONDITION)
- What are the indicators of the learner's successful accomplishment of the objective? (DEGREE OR STANDARD)

In the following sections, audience, behavior, condition, and degree (or standard) will be defined and discussed in detail.

Audience

The audience is who the learners are (office managers, police officers, firefighters, etc.). Conducting an audience analysis (described more fully in Chapter 6) will ensure that you know your learners. The learner information necessary to develop good instruction includes their reading ability, past training, job rating, special needs, age, etc.

Behavior

In the context of writing instructional objectives, the definition of *behavior* is as follows:

> The behavioral component of an instructional objective specifies what the learner must do, produce, or perform in order to demonstrate achievement of the instructional objective.

It is extremely important that the behavior included in the objective be expressed clearly. The learner and the instructor must have the same idea or definition in mind concerning what must be done.

Use Action Verbs

When you write the "behavior" part of an instructional objective, use action verbs to specify behavior that is observable and measurable (see Figure 4-4). Measurement is difficult if behavioral objectives are described with verbs such as "appreciate," "understand," "internalize," etc. In these cases, how would you really know if someone had learned what has been taught? On the other hand, "doing" words can more precisely describe what is expected of the learners in the "behavior" area. Remember Gagné's five categories of learned capabilities (or behavior). You must decide which kind of behavioral performance is required and use the appropriate verb. The action verb must always match the kind of learning capability desired.

Record the required behavior of your instructional objective in a form that will enable your learners to demonstrate the learned behaviors you wish them to exhibit. For example, if you wish your learners to recognize all the parts of a certain valve, write the objective as follows:

> Given a picture containing twenty-five (25) parts from various valves, circle *only* the parts pertaining to Brand X gate valves. *All* Brand X parts must be circled within five (5) minutes.

In this instance, you want your learners to memorize all the parts of Brand X gate valves, recognize them by sight, know how many parts there are, and differentiate these parts from other valve parts not of the Brand X-type. If your learners can successfully complete the objective as written, you can be certain they have the required knowledge.

Sample Action Verbs

Capability	Key Verb	Other Possible Verbs
Intellectual Skills		
• Discrimination	Discriminate	Match, Classify, Combine, Organize
• Concrete Concept	Identify	Name, Distinguish, List
• Defined Concept	Classify	Define, Discuss, Reorder, Correct, Outline, Contrast, Compare, Appraise
• Rule	Demonstrate	Solve, Translate, Calculate, Evaluate, Estimate
• Higher Order Rule	Generate	Synthesize, Explain, Formulate, Create, Improve, Devise
Cognitive Strategy	Adopt	Select, Analyze, Modify, Reorder, Rearrange, Predict, Propose, Plan, Project
Verbal Information	State	List, Recall, Record
Motor Skill	Execute	Manipulate, Tie, Hold, Assemble, Raise, Draw, Knock-down, Operate, Search, Replace, Drive, Twist
Attitude	Choose	Compare, Decide, Act

Figure 4-4.

One or more of the five senses can detect the performance of a behavior. If you can outwardly detect and judge a learner's performance by a simple physical observation, that performance is, in essence, the test. If the required behavior were to bake an apple pie, the learner's performance would be the finished product. The pie could be judged by appearance, taste, smell, texture, weight, and shape. No "indicators" would be needed to demonstrate hidden performance.

In teaching technical skills it has proven useful to approach instructional objective writing and decision making from another perspective (Cantor, 1990; Montague et al., 1983).

Here are five classes or categories of instructional objectives to consider, based on the types of tasks to be performed by your learner.

- Remember
- Use, unaided transfer
- Use, aided transfer
- Use, unaided no transfer
- Use, aided no transfer

First, review your job/task analysis data and determine if your learner is to *remember* or *use* the learned information to do something. These two objectives differ about what your learner must do. The distinction corresponds to the difference between knowledge and application.

An example follows below.

- *Remember*—Your learner will write the formula for calculating conversion from Celsius to Fahrenheit temperature.
- *Use*—Your learner will set up a defibrillator to resuscitate a patient.

The remember/use distinction is a simple one; on its basis analyze the action in both the instructional objective and associated test item(s). The chart in Figure 4-5 above lists

Remember/Use Action Verb Chart

Remember	Use	
Name	Apply	Operate
State (from memory)	Remove	Repair
List (from memory)	Analyze	Adjust
Recall	Derive	Calibrate
Remember	Demonstrate	Replace
Write (from memory)	Evaluate	Assemble
Recognize	Solve	Disassemble
Explain (from memory)	Prove	Calculate
Select	Sort	Troubleshoot
Describe	Maintain	Load
Identify	Compute	Predict
	Determine	Unload

Figure 4-5.

appropriate verbs to describe the two categories. Select the verb appropriate to your instructional intent.

For those tasks calling for use, now determine which ones indicate *unaided* versus *aided* use. An *unaided* use objective requires learners to perform the task with no help other than their own memory. An aided use objective allows learners to perform the task with help from sources other than memory. You must specify the job aid(s) to be used in the performance. The basic rule again: anything that replaces the need for memory will count as an aid, including, for example:

- a list of procedure steps from a shop manual;
- a formula for problem solving; and,
- a requirement for a field supervisor's guidance.

Key Words for No-Transfer Level Instructional Objectives

Apply	Remove
Operate	Replace
Repair	Assemble
Adjust	Produce
Calibrate	Destroy

Figure 4-6.

Next, you must determine which of the *use* objectives are no-transfer versus transfer. A no-transfer instructional objective requires your learner to perform a specific procedural task the same way every time—an ordered sequence of steps. The learner does not have to transfer or generalize performance to new situations. A no-transfer instructional objective can be either aided or unaided. Key words in no-transfer instructional objectives include those in Figure 4-6. The following are additional examples of *no-transfer* objectives:

Type a letter within 30 minutes.

Remove a ribbon from a typewriter.

Transfer level instructional objectives may be applied in a variety of situations. In other words, knowledge will be used to meet new problems that will be related but not identical to previous ones. Key words that might be seen in transfer level instructional objectives are given in Figure 4-7. The following are additional examples of objectives at the *transfer* level.

The learner will calculate total stopping distance of a vehicle moving at 60 miles-per-hour.

Key Words for Transfer Level Instructional Objectives

Solve	Find
Derive	Translate
Prove	Program
Calculate	Add
Troubleshoot	Subtract

Notice that transfer level objectives may be use aided or unaided.

Figure 4-7.

> Given the formula for gasoline engine displacement, instruction on how to apply it, and the values of a cylinder bore and piston length from a manual, the learner will calculate cubic inch displacement.

Remember that both no-transfer and transfer level instructional objectives may be aided or unaided. In this analysis of the task the important factor is the ultimate behavior performance of your learners.

In summary, there are three tasks in classifying an objective for teaching technical skills.

- Determine if your learner is to remember or use the information to be taught.

- If your learner is to use the information, determine if the task is to be performed unaided, from memory alone, or aided, by various devices.

- If your learner is to use the information, determine whether the task is a no-transfer situation in which the job is always the same or involves the transfer of information to a new situation.

These concepts will prove useful to you in monitoring the effectiveness of your instruction, and in performing lesson or course evaluation (as will be described in Chapter 9).

Some Performance Statement Pitfalls

Consider the behavior statement in the following objective:

> Develop in the learners a critical understanding of the importance of effective management.

This might describe what you want to happen, but the instructional objective is poorly stated for the following reasons:

- First, the instructional objective is stated in terms of what the instructor wants to do. An instructional objective is supposed to state learner performance at the end of training, *not* the instructor's actions or intent.
- The terms "critical understanding" and "effective management" are not defined, and hence would be very difficult to measure.

Condition

When it is to be part of an instructional objective, the definition of *condition* is as follows:

> The *condition* component of an instructional objective indicates the actual circumstances or givens—the specifications and/or limitations that are inherent or imposed when your learners demonstrate their mastery of the objective.

When learners know under what conditions they must perform the learned behavior, they know much more specifically what is required of them and can study and/or prepare accordingly.

Examples of Conditions

Listed below are good examples of "conditions" that may be included as part of specific objectives:

- Given a list of...
- Given any reference of the learner's choice...
- Given a standard set of tools...
- Given a properly functioning pump...
- Without the aid of a slide rule or calculator...
- Without the aid of tools...
- Using the text as a reference...
- In a high radiation area...
- Under emergency conditions...

While teaching a course in algebra you might write an instructional objective such as:

> The learners will be able to solve problems in algebra.

More specific wording would be something like this:

> Given a linear equation with one unknown, learners will be able to solve (write the solution) for the unknown without the aid of references, tables, or calculating devices.

As written above, this instructional objective (Mager, 1984; Blank, 1982) contains detailed and specific information on the parameters of the problem for the student, who now knows exactly what must be mastered. In addition, these kinds of clear instructional objectives help the instructor decide how best to teach the subject and how to devise accurate evaluation instruments.

Sometimes, constructing or examining a sample test item will help clarify the conditions necessary for an objective to be reached. Here are two examples:

Objective: Given standard equipment, the student will be able to start an intravenous (I.V.) injection in the arm of a patient.

Test Item: Start an I.V. on any member of the class within two (2) tries.

Objective: Be able to solve simple linear equations in one unknown.

Test Item: Solve for x in the following:
a. $2 + 4x = 12$
b. $9x - 3 = 6$

You will not always find it necessary to use example test items as an aid. However, if you find it difficult to clarify the condition of an objective, you may find it useful to write such an item in order to see more clearly what is required and thus make your specifications more precise.

Are Conditions Always Necessary?

When you prepare an instructional objective for which you are sure that the conditions under which the learners are to perform are completely obvious, you may exclude the condition. For example, for the objective, "Write the six (6) factors that control the Effective Multiplication Factor in nuclear fission," it would be unnecessary to add the condition, "given a pencil and paper"!

However, not including conditions *must* be an exception to the normal rule. When a condition is not specified, ask another instructor and a few learners to read the objective. If any one of them is unsure of the conditions under which the task is to be performed, write them down. When in doubt, include the condition in your written objective.

When deciding what to include in the "condition" part of your objective, ask yourself these questions.

- What will the learner be allowed to use (tools, references, etc.)?
- What will the learner be denied?
- Under what adverse physical or mental conditions will the learner be expected to demonstrate performance?
- Are there any skills which I am *not* trying to develop?

When answering these questions, if any point seems important or unclear, write a condition in your objective.

Degree or Standard

The definition of degree or standard is as follows:

> The degree or standard component of an objective indicates the desired behavioral performance level your learners must attain to be considered successful.

Notice that the words "desired behavioral performance level" are used. This does not imply minimum or barely acceptable criteria. The desired performance is the level the learner *must* reach in order to be proficient.

Are Standards Always Important or Possible?

Well-written instructional objectives are very clear. A degree or standard must be included to further strengthen and clarify the "behavior" part of the objective. If your learners can see what they are to do and how well they must do it, they can plan their efforts more efficiently. Also, it will be clearer to you, as the instructor, what the learners must do to show competence. Evaluation of the learners will be much easier and less time-consuming if you have a degree or standard to use when observing learner behavioral performance (see Chapter 5).

Some subjects require the mastery of objectives that are abstract and intangible, and cognitive or knowledge-oriented. You may think that it is extremely difficult (if not impossible) to construct a definite standard for such objectives. In many situations intangibles or abstract concepts can be analyzed and broken down to the point where they become concrete and open to measurement. In order to do this, you must think of behavioral performances that define knowledge goals (such words as "list," "state," "write," "define," etc.). These performances can be measured in terms of quality and/or quantity. When you accomplish this, you then can put a standard in your instructional objective. For example:

> Define the term "New Economy" and provide three examples to which it would be applied.

Types of Degrees or Standards

The standard of an objective falls into one of three general classifications.
- Speed
- Quality
- Quantity

(If you do not intend to evaluate a behavior performance on the basis of speed, you should not impose a time limit. Only impose those criteria that are important; do not use a time standard as a "filter" in your objectives.)

Speed

A common component of an acceptable performance is the designation of a time limit within which the given behavior must occur. When you tell learners how long an examination period will be, you are setting a time standard. If speed of accomplishment is important in an objective, be open and honest about it. When learners know that time is important, they will be able to practice with that in mind and perform as intended. For example, an objective may read:

- Analyze a blood sample for type and white blood cell count within 7 minutes; or,
- Fire the entire ten-round magazine within 30 seconds, obtaining a minimum score of 30 points.

In both of the above instructional objectives, time becomes an important limit and a standard for measurement. To attain these instructional objectives successfully, your learners will need to practice so that they can work quickly enough. Thus, the time standard can act as a motivator to encourage more effective learning, as well as clearly define performance. This is true of all the three types of degrees or standards.

Quality

Sometimes, how well something is done is more important than speed. If your learners know the degree of precision required in a certain performance, they can plan how much effort or practice will be necessary to obtain the required accuracy. The following are examples of quality standards:

- Solutions must be accurate to the nearest whole number.
- Machine the shaft to within ±.002 inches diameter of the technical manual specification.
- The estimated critical position shall be within ±6 steps of actual critical rod position.

Quality of the performance or finished product may be the critical consideration. Quality usually involves comparing the finished product to a given physical example of perfection.

For example, you want your learners to draw a six-inch (6") diameter circle freehand and you want the circle to be "round." In emphasizing the roundness of the circle, you might say "very round" or "really round" or "almost perfectly round."

Your learner would still not be sure how to visualize acceptable performance. In the following example, the amount of roundness is clear to your learner and to the evaluator.

> Without the aid of a compass, the learners will be able to draw a six-inch (6") diameter circle freehand. When compared to a compass-drawn six-inch (6") template, the learners' circles will vary no more than 1/8" from the outer edge of the template.

If you write a quality degree or standard in an objective, you will have to give a physical example of the desired performance, or provide a list of behavioral performance traits that can be objectively evaluated in order to show the learner exactly what you want.

Quantity

An obvious way to measure performance is to require a certain number of items or certain amount of one substance to be produced. Sometimes you may combine quantity with speed.

- Correctly solve at least five (5) of eight (8) math problems.
- Install twenty-three (23) automobile alternators per day.
- X-ray three (3) patients per hour, with no errors.

Pointing to the Standard

You can indicate a standard in an objective without actually describing it. This idea is called "pointing" to the standard. There are basically five ways of pointing.

(1) If an intended standard is stated *very clearly* in an available document, add words to the instructional objective that tells where to find the document. For example:

- ...as per 1982 Chevy Chevette shop manual, pp. 59–63;
- ...according to the Machinist's Standards Chart, 1981 edition;
- ...in the sequence listed in Technical Staff Procedure 43A.

(2) If the performance consists of a number of steps, you might point to an evaluation checklist as the degree or standard. When the checklist is available to your learners, they can tell how well and in what sequence the steps must be done.

(3) Another way to point to the standard is by referring learners to a film or a videotape and saying, in effect, "Do it like that." This method must be used with caution, for it is easily misinterpreted with unexpected results. Be sure the tape or film is an accurate example of the desired performance. You should carefully describe the characteristics of the film or tape you wish the learners to copy.

(4) Another way is to specify the overall performance that must be achieved on a written or oral test of cognitive-type objectives. This is particularly useful when a large number of objectives are being evaluated on the same test. This method does *not* evaluate each and every objective in a pass/fail manner. It evaluates them as a collective group using such criteria as: "No section to obtain less than 70% score, with at least an 80% average score overall." The creation of examination questions from knowledge behavioral objectives is not an easy task.

(5) Standards can sometimes be indicated in objectives by the use of important performance verbs, such as "state," "discuss," and "explain." Defining these performances can facilitate writing exam questions. This can enhance the validity of the tests, since test questions will be covered by a behavioral objective. Also, the instructional objective will be tested to the

proper level. Definitions of "state," "discuss," and "explain" are included here to clarify these terms.

- *State.* Means that learners are expected to recall specific details, universal rules or principles, patterns, structures, or settings. Memorization is key here, and this level of response represents the verbal or factual information category in the classes of *previously learned capabilities*.

- *Discuss.* Means that learners are expected to produce in-depth information that will demonstrate comprehensive understanding of the knowledge or skills described in this objective. To "discuss" assesses the learners' comprehension of subject and ability to apply knowledge to new situations.

- *Explain.* Means that learners are expected to provide in-depth information that demonstrates comprehensive understanding of the knowledge or skills described in this instructional objective. Learners must demonstrate mastery of this level with *no* prompting or leading from the instructor. They will be expected to provide supporting data and/or drawings.

Instructional objectives using all three of these verbs are most appropriate for training where oral evaluations are given.

Summary

In this chapter, I have discussed the use and writing of instructional objectives. Instructional objectives are precise, clear, and complete statements concerning what your learners will be able to do at the end of your training sessions. In other words, instructional objectives clearly define the *acceptable* performance learners must exhibit to be classified as successful.

You now know how to write instructional objectives. You know that describing the *audience, behavior, condition,* and *degree or standard* enables you to be very clear about what you want your learners to learn and how well you want them to learn it. To remind you once more of these four (4) parts of an objective, they are defined as follows:

- AUDIENCE: States exactly who the intended learners are.
- BEHAVIOR: States exactly what you want the learner to do.
- CONDITION: Specifies givens, restrictions, and physical restraints under which the task is to be performed.
- DEGREE or STANDARD: Gives the precision with which something must be done in order to be considered successful.

And, as a final word, here, again, are the important benefits of training objectives:

- Learners are able to learn more easily.
- Instructors are able to teach more effectively.
- Training becomes more standardized.
- Training becomes easier to document.
- Evaluation becomes easier and more efficient.

Chapter References

Blank, W. (1982). *Handbook for developing competency-based training programs.* Englewood Cliffs, NJ: Prentice-Hall, 261-374.

Cantor, J. A. (1990, April). How to perform a comprehensive course evaluation.
Performance and Instruction, 8-15.

Cantor, J. A. (1988, January). A new dimension in military instructional development. *Performance and Instruction*, 14-20.

Cantor, J. A. (1986a). A systems approach to instructional development in technical education. *Journal of Studies in Technical Careers*, 9 (2), Spring, 155-166.

Cantor, J. A. (1986b). The Delphi as a job analysis tool. *Journal of Instructional Development*, 9 (1), 16-19.

Cantor, J.A. (2000a). *Higher Education Outside of the Academy. 2000 Report.* Vol. 27, Number 7. ASHE-ERIC Higher Education Reports - 2000. The ERIC Clearninghouse on Higher Education. Washington, DC: The George Washington University, Graduate School of Education and Human Development.

Cross, P. K. (1981). *Adults as learners: Increasing participation and facilitating learning*. San Francisco, CA: Jossey-Bass Inc.

Dick, W. W., & Carey, L. (1978). *The systematic design of instruction*. Glenview, IL.: Scott, Foresman.

Heinrich, R., Molenda, M., Russell, J. & Smaldino, S. (2002). *Instructional Media and Technologies for Learning*, 7th ed. Englewood Cliffs, NJ: Prentice-Hall.

Knowles, M. S. (1980, February). "Malcolm Knowles on...'Some thoughts about environment and learning—Educational ecology, if you like.'" *Training and Development Journal*, 34-36.

Mager, R. F. (1984). *Preparing instructional objectives,* 2nd ed. Belmont, CA: Lake.

Montague, W. E., Ellis, J. A. , & Wulfeck, W. H. (1983). *The instructional quality inventory (IQI): A formative evaluation tool for instructional systems development* (Monograph). San Diego, CA: Navy Personnel Research & Development Center.

National Fire Academy. (1989). *Fire service instructional methodology*. Emmitsburg, MD: Author.

Spaid, O. (1986). *The consummate trainer: A practitioner's perspective*. Reston, VA: Reston Publishing, 1-64.

United States Army, Corps of Engineers. (1982). *Instructional Methods*. Washington, DC: unpublished.

United States Department of Defense. (1975). *Interservice Procedures for Instructional Systems Development* (NAVEDTRA 106A). Washington, DC: Author.

United States Department of the Navy. (1976). *Training specifications manual (Naval Air Maintenance Training Group)*. Washington, DC: unpublished.

United States Department of Labor. (1972). *Handbook for analyzing jobs*. Washington, DC: Government Printing Office.

Walls, R. T., Haught, P. A., & Dowler D. L. (1982). *How to train new skills: Planning, teaching, evaluating*. Dunbar, WV: Research and Training Center Press.

5

Instructional Evaluation and Test Development

Ask your learners probing, high-level questions to promote independent thought.

The process of instructional evaluation is a useful and necessary tool for you, the instructor, and your learners. Through evaluation, the instructional value of a lesson or course is assessed. It must, therefore, be linked directly to instructional objectives.

Evaluation provides the information necessary to determine your degree of instructional success (a formative assessment). In addition, this feedback is useful in planning future lessons (summative evaluation). Evaluation also provides a yardstick against which to measure learner improvement and helps ensure that training is on target for the identified audience and need. Finally, evaluation can serve as evidence if litigation should subsequently occur (Baird et al., 1985).

For the learner, evaluation can: (1) serve as feedback to guide study and indicate progress; (2) provide evidence of suitability for promotion (e.g. certification); and (3) ensure that, as an employee, the learner is capable of carrying out a task safely. (Baird et al., 1985; Driscoll, 1994, adds to the science on educational evaluation.)

Categories of Evaluation

The evaluation processes in your instructional program should be both formative and summative (Dick & Carey, 1978). *Formative evaluation* is ongoing assessment carried out throughout the training. It is used to determine progress and/or weakness in instruction both before and during its implementation. Formative evaluation should take place at all stages of course development and delivery (Dick & Carey, 1978; Driscoll, 1994). Basically, it involves constantly asking questions of yourself and others during various stages of the instructional process.

- Before determining instructional objectives, ask: Why is this instruction being developed? What instructional objectives should be developed? What types of activities are needed?

- While teaching, ask: Am I maintaining the original instructional purpose? Is the instruction suitable for the learners' needs? Are the learners responding as expected? Are they learning?

- After the lesson or course is over, ask: Did the learners learn and did I instruct properly?

Formative evaluation measures include pretests, oral questioning, performance quizzes, and instructional activities. Also included can be questionnaires, observations, class participation, and oral presentations. Questionnaires are useful in various learning situations; however, make sure that learners take the time to complete each item carefully. Observations, like all anecdotal records, are only as effective as the observer; however, this method of assessment is valuable for getting a "gut reaction" to instruction. Class participation is another subjective formative evaluation measure. Oral presentations provide indicators of progress made, especially if the course contains more than one such presentation. Checking the results of a follow-up test on a lesson against the instructional objectives, conducting pretests, and field-testing a pilot course (which assesses the instruction before it is formally implemented [see Chapter 9]) also provide formative evaluation.

Summative evaluation measures the degree to which the lesson or course has met its intended goal and whether or not your learners can actually perform the requirements of the job. Examples of summative measures are overall course reviews, as well as overall assessments of personnel job readiness over specific periods of time.

Evaluation processes, in particular, the development of written and performance tests, will be discussed in this chapter; and in Chapter 9, lesson, course, and instructor evaluation processes will be described.

Methods for Written Test Development

Evaluation is the cornerstone of the training and development process. It is the means by which we make sure that we, as effective instructors, are actually teaching what we should be teaching and are doing so effectively. Evaluation measures the worth of our process and helps determine our own value as instructors. It is for this reason that we develop test items and tests immediately following the design and development of learning objectives (Cantor, 1987a). Most evaluation involves the use of some type of test to determine how well learners have mastered the instructional material presented to them. There are many different kinds of tests, including written, performance, and oral. Written tests can consist of test items developed in several forms: multiple-choice, true-false, matching, completion-type, short-answer, and essay.

Writing Multiple-Choice Test Items

The multiple-choice test is by far the most popular format for written tests, because it can determine mastery of many different subject areas and can assess a variety of intellectual processes from information recall to cognitive strategies. Multiple-choice tests consist of a series of questions or test items. Each test item measures a particular behavior, providing specific information on what a learner knows about a specific topic. To be valid and accurate, a good test must rely on well-written items. Test item writing is an art. No single set of rules can ensure good test items, but some general principles can help. Your skill in applying these principles will determine the quality of the test items and, as a result, the integrity of the test as a useful measurement instrument. Successful test item writers possess a unique combination of abilities. They know the subject matter, understand educationally and psychologically the target population taking the test, and are skilled communicators.[1]

Format for Multiple-Choice Test Items

A multiple-choice test item consists of two parts, a stem and a set of responses, one of which is correct and three of which are distractors. Figure 5-1 displays a typical multiple-choice test item.

The stem has one central theme, in this case the nature of a claw hammer. It asks a question, presents a problem, or takes the form of an incomplete statement. Most instructors, as test item writers, prefer this latter item form because it presents the central theme clearly and because it avoids tipping off, or cuing, the correct answer. The distractors list possible answers to the question or problem; here they provide a variety of choices about possible uses of a claw hammer. Notice that the correct answer and the three distractors are similar in grammatical structure.

This illustrates a crucial point: all distractors must be plausible as correct responses, and they must be written in a way that

1 Portions of this section originally appeared in J. A. Cantor, Developing multiple-choice test items. *Training & Development Journal* 1987, May, 85-88.

Example of Multiple-Choice Test Item

What is a claw hammer?   (stem)

     a. A woodworking tool.   (correct)

     b. A metalworking tool.   (distractor)

     c. An autobody tool.   (distractor)

     d. A sheetmetal tool.   (distractor)

Figure 5-1.

prevents learners from guessing the proper answer simply on the basis of their format.

If, for example, Distractor A read, "A handle implement with a metallic striking surface used for pounding nails into and removing nails from wood or wood-composite materials," learners probably would have little difficulty choosing it as the correct response. It is so different from the other distractors that it cues itself. Similarly, if Distractor B said, "A type of nuclear reactor," learners would probably rule it out, because it is not plausible compared to the other distractors.

Knowing this basic format—a stem with one central theme and four responses, including three similar and plausible distractors—can help you get started on good multiple-choice test item construction. But before you can begin writing any test items, you have to decide what sort of information the test should cover.

Central Themes and Possible Distractors

You need to identify the central themes to be tested. You will be at least generally familiar with the subject taught, and you may have developed the course materials yourself. Go back to the documents that formed the basis of the instruction: the job or task analysis, objectives, content specifications, and lesson plans. Use these documents to identify the aspects, concepts, facts, and the like that are essential for mastery of the subject matter. These critical skills or knowledge form the core of your test; each of them represents a possible central theme for a test item.

Now ask yourself a few questions. How can the learner demonstrate knowledge of this theme? In what sort of circumstances might it be important to understand these concepts? If a learner did not know or understand these concepts or facts, what might be the consequences? What common misconceptions do workers have about this subject? These questions and their answers help you fine-tune the nature of the test items and the manner in which you will construct them.

For example, suppose the subject is emergency medical care, and your course design documents tell you it is critical to know how to treat shock. You might ask yourself, "If someone did not know the proper treatment for shock, what steps might that person take?" Write down the answers that occur to you and then add the correct response to your list. This makes a good preliminary set of distractors.

At this stage, do not worry too much about proper wording or format; you are only trying to create a first draft of the test item.

Write out the stem, making sure it presents a discrete central theme. Although the following figure asks its question in two separate sentences, it has one central theme: What should you do to treat someone who is in shock? Now, arrange all your distractors, including the correct response, below the stem and letter them consecutively. If more than the needed four occur to you, put them down anyway. You can decide later, which are the best. Now you have a base from which to construct your final version of the item.

Example of the Correct-Answer Form of a Multiple-Choice Test Item

An accident victim is in shock. Which one of the following actions should be taken?

    a. Cover the victim to keep him/her warm. (Correct)

    b. Raise the victim's head above the knees.

    c. Postition victim's head on a pillow.

    d. Put an ice pack on the victim's head.

    e. Position the victim so he/she is lying on his/her back.

Figure 5-2.

Item Format and Stem Revision

Multiple-choice items commonly take four forms: *correct answer*, *best answer*, *negative*, and *combined-response*. The type of item you select will depend on the material to be tested and the complexity of the processes that indicate a learner's mastery. In general, though, the simpler and clearer the item, the better the test.

The *correct-answer* form simply asks a question and requires the examinee to choose the correct response. One answer is absolutely correct while the others are incorrect, as shown in Figure 5-2.

The stem asks a straightforward question, based on a well-defined central theme, and your learner selects an answer from the list of distractors. This item format works best for testing unambiguous facts, where there is little room for debate about the correctness of the response. Learners can either recall the information or they cannot.

The correct-answer format also lends itself to completion items such as "Columbus discovered America in…" In this type of test item, the distractors complete the sentence begun in the stem.

The *best-answer* format involves slightly more complex thinking processes, because it presents more than one "correct" distractor. Your learners must select the best or most nearly correct answer. Some or all of the distractors may be appropriate in varying degrees, but only one of them is the correct response. Figure 5-3 demonstrates one way of using the best-answer format.

The best-answer format works well here because the primary goal of a police force cannot be stated with irrefutable precision; it is a matter subject to some debate. However, your learners' instruction would no doubt emphasize one primary goal, and this test item asks them to recall it.

Even if the instruction did not explicitly state the answer to this question, the item still may be valid if the training gave your learner enough information to evaluate this issue and draw the appropriate conclusions. However, you should try to avoid this problem whenever possible by including additional clarifying information in the stem. The item in the above figure could be restated like this: "According to Kane's analysis in *Police Science*, which of the following is the fundamental purpose of law enforcement in the US?" The specific reference to a source with which your learner should be familiar eliminates any

---

Example of the Best-Answer Form of a Multiple-Choice Test Item

What is the fundamental purpose of law enforcement in the United States?

    a. To arrest criminals.

    b. To maintain order without a loss of liberty. (Correct)

    c. To control citizen conduct though the imparial enforcement of detectable violations.

    d. To achieve a balanced program of criminal and civil enforcement.

Figure 5-3.

ambiguities that might cause confusion and invalidate the item. In all best-answer items, make sure that all competent experts would agree on the "best answer."

The *negative* form instructs your learner to choose the answer that is incorrect. The distractors include three true answers and one that is incorrect or definitely weaker than the others. That's the one your learners are supposed to select. Figure 5-4 gives an example of the negative form.

Negative items are appropriate when knowing the exception is as important as knowing the rule. However, take special care to avoid confusing your learners. Do not use double negatives, such as a negative stem with instructions to find the exception. An example of this poor pattern would be this rewording of the item in Figure 5-4: "None of the following are undesirable practices when preparing multiple-choice items except:" That construction is unnecessarily complicated, and your learners' correct answers may tell you more about their patience in decoding difficult material than about their understanding of the central theme. You can also help steer your learners in the right direction by underlining or capitalizing the negative qualifier, which in this case was "*except.*"

The *combined-response* form uses a stem followed by several numbered answer choices, one or more of which may

Example of the Negative Form of a Multiple-Choice Test Item

All of the following are desirable practices when preparing multiple-choice items except:

    a. stating the stem positively.

    b. using a stem suitable for a short-answer item.

    c. underlining certain words in the stem for emphasis.

    d. shortening the stem by lengthening the distractors. (Correct)

Figure 5-4.

Example of the Combined-Response Form of a Multiple-Choice Test Item

An officer posed with a life-threatening situation discharged her service revolver. Her partner had drawn his weapon, but had not fired it. Two other officers were present at the discharge and had drawn their weapons. Three more officers reported to the scene after the discharge. The weapon(s) of which individual(s) listed below should be preserved for processing.

1. The officer who discharged the service revolver.

2. The partner who drew his weapon.

3. The two officers who were present at the discharge and who drew their weapons.

4. The three officers who arrived after the discharge.

     a. 1 only.

     b. 1 and 2 only. (Correct)

     c. 1, 2, and 3 only.

     d. 1, 2, 3, and 4.

Figure 5-5.

be correct. A second set of code letters lists various possible combinations of correct responses. Your learner chooses the *letter* that designates the correct response or responses, as in Figure 5-5. You can also use the combined-response form to ask the learner to rearrange material in sequences such as chronological order, order of importance, and the like.

The combined-response form is a difficult one for both the item writer and your learner. However, it permits the assessment of higher order intellectual skills, such as organizational ability and the ability to evaluate facts and concepts. Exercise care, though, to keep it from becoming a multiple "true/false" item.

No matter which format you choose for your test items and their stems, keep a few general rules in mind. Include only one central theme in each stem. This lets the learners zero in on the

---

Example of Incorrect Shortening of the Stem

George Washington was the:

    a. *first* man to cross the Deleware River.

    b. *first* member of Congress.

    c. *first* president of the United States. (Correct)

    d. *first* general in the Continental Army.

Figure 5-6.

exact information you seek. Word each stem as clearly and concisely as possible to avoid confusion. If there are any words or phrases common to all responses, place them instead in the stem. Include in the stem any qualifying words that limit or isolate the possible responses. Take a look at Figure 5-6.

In Figure 5-6 above, the italicized word *first*, which appears at the beginning of each distractor, belongs in the stem. Thus the stem should read: "George Washington was the first:" This construction lets learners know right away that they need to recall something that Washington did *first*.

Developing and Writing Distractors

Now you have a good stem, a correct response, and a preliminary list of distractors. Review that list again, remembering that all distractors must be plausible and must fit the grammatical structure of the stem. Some general guidelines can help you revise your choices.

First of all, avoid using "none of the above" or "all of the above" as distractors. They are often confusing. Also avoid obviously incorrect responses. Both of these devices destroy plausibility.

To make sure your distractors are plausible, define the class of things to which all of the answer choices should belong. For example, go back to Figure 5-2, the item that asks what you should do to treat someone in shock. The class of possible answers might be defined as "first-aid measures." This process gives you distractors B, D, and E, which seem like valid first-aid procedures.

Now think of things more specifically associated with the terms stated in the stem and consider some common misconceptions people may hold about the subject in question. Now, you have distractor C; an uninformed person might think the most important factor is making the victim comfortable. Thus, all the distractors in Figure 5-2 are plausible. Since most test items contain only three distractors plus the correct response, you can throw out one of the distractors.

Remember to write distractors so they make grammatical sense. That means making them correspond to the syntactic structure of the stem. Be sure that the beginning of each distractor logically follows the last word in the stem. For example, if the stem ends with the word "an," your learners will probably assume that the correct response is a singular noun beginning with a vowel; make very sure all the distractors have this pattern. When using items that ask your learners to complete a sentence, as in Figure 5-6, ensure that all the distractors do, in fact, complete the sentence. Also note in that figure that all the distractors begin with lower-case letters and end with a period.

Finally, place all distractors in logical order if they are numerically or sequentially related.

Remember that, like stems, the most effective distractors are clearly and concisely written without excess information that could confuse the examinee. Keep in mind that a good test item measures your learners' ability to recall a central theme or solve a particular problem, etc., not their ability to take tests.

Examples of True/False Test Items

☐ A "water hammer" occurs when the direction of flow through a fire hose or main water line is suddenly stopped or reversed. (True)

☐ A "water hammer" occurs when the discharge volume of a fire stream is suddenly increased. (False)

Figure 5-7.

Writing True/False Test Items

True/false test items are effective for testing mastery of content. These tests are limited, however, since they can only test for factual information. Although true/false statements are usually fairly easy to write, they must be entirely true or entirely false. Ambiguities can lead to arguments with learners over validity. Avoid specific determiners such as "always," "none," "never," or "all." Make sure all statements are plausible. Figure 5-7 above presents an example of two possible true/false test items.

Writing Matching Test Items

Matching test items can condense the testing of a relatively large amount of information. Matching tests require information sequencing and assimilating. If the facts are selected carefully, the chance of guessing is greatly reduced. The disadvantages are that matching test items cannot effectively test higher order intellectual skills, and their content must have relational association (e.g. cause and effect, term and definition).

Matching test items (Figure 5-8) are related to multiple-choice test items in that many of the latter can be combined into one matching test item. Matching tests are good for testing content that includes classifying, sequencing,

Example of Matching Test Item

DIRECTIONS: Match the type of test on the left with the disadvantage of using that method on the right.

__ 1. Multiple-Choice

__ 2. True/False

__ 3. Matching

__ 4. Short Answer

__ 5. Essay

a. Can't test higher level of learning.

b. Takes time to construct effective test.

c. Questions can be too broad or ambiguous.

d. Can only test factual information.

e. Questions must be carefully phrased to lead student to a specific answer.

Figure 5-8.

labeling, or defining (defined concepts). Although matching items are an acceptable method of evaluation, avoid their overuse.

In structuring matching test items, give directions that describe the matching task to be performed. Use a set of 4 to 12 problems or terms. Place the terms on the left and the alternative responses on the right; capitalize the first letter of the word in each item to identify where it starts. All components of a given matching item should be contained on a single page to avoid flipping back and forth between pages.

A well-constructed matching test item contains clear instructions stating how the items are to be matched and whether responses are to be used only once. Each question should have a central theme with parallel problems and parallel responses. This parallelism will help prevent guessing. If used, distractors should be plausible. Make sure there are no grammatical clues (e.g. "a" or "an") given in the items. Arrange alternatives in logical order, for instance, alphabetically or numerically. This ordering makes it easier to locate alternatives and reduces the chance of giving subtle clues.

Writing Short-Answer/Completion Test Items

Short-answer/completion test items enable a large amount of information to be evoked by a few questions. Because learners must actually respond in their own words in writing, you can make a clearer assessment of what has been learned. These items are limited to recall of specific facts, however. Also, the items must be carefully phrased to avoid directing the learner to a specific answer.

Short-answer/completion test items are easy to construct and may be used to test recall of specific facts, concepts, or principles (Figure 5-9). When constructing completion items, be certain that there is only one answer that will complete the statement. Answers should require no more than a few words; if more are needed, it will be hard to mark the answers objectively.

A common structure for the short-answer/completion test item is an incomplete statement. In this formulation, a significant word (or two) is left out and the learner must complete the

---

Example of Short-Answer Test Item

List the steps performed in connecting a hose to a fire hydrant.

1. _____

2. _____

3. _____

4. _____

Figure 5-9.

Example of Completion Test Item

The name of the President of the United States in 1987 was

_____

Figure 5-10.

statement. Another type of completion test requires the recall of the name of something. Yet another form of short-answer test requires the learners to compile a list. Statements should be simple and straightforward, with the blanks appearing at or near the end of the statement.

In well-constructed short-answer/completion items, each item is matched to an objective. A clear, complete statement is provided. No grammatical clues are given. Figure 5-10 is a completion test item.

Writing Essay Test Items

Essay test items (Figure 5-11) can test for higher order intellectual skills and cognitive strategies. They allow your learners to display mastery of an entire range of knowledge about a subject. There are, however, several disadvantages associated with essay tests. For one thing, it is often difficult to write question items that are not too broad or ambiguous; this in turn makes scoring difficult. Also, only a limited number of concepts and principles can be tested. Essay tests are not fair to participants with poor writing skills. Finally, from the instructor's point of view, essays are much more time-consuming to grade.

While essay test items are excellent for evaluating higher levels of learning and application of principles, they are very difficult to construct in such a way as to limit subjectivity. In a

---

Example of Essay Test Item

Discuss the four primary advantages of incident command and compare these advantages to the alternatives of not using an incidental command system.

(Each advantage and alternative discussed will be worth up to 4 points.)

Figure 5-11.

well-constructed essay test, complete directions are given, questions are clearly and unambiguously written, model responses are used in grading, and components and their weighting are identified. Ample space is also provided for the answer or directions are given for using additional space. Allow learners plenty of time to formulate and construct their answers.

Reviewing Your Test Items

Now that you have fine-tuned your draft item, regardless of the type and whatever the format, you need to review it. Ask yourself the following questions (Cantor, 1987b):

- Does the item truly measure what I am trying to measure?

- Will the intent of the item be clear to someone reading it for the first time?

- Do my learners have all of the information they need to answer the item?

- Is the wording as clear and concise as possible? If not, can the item be revised and still be understood?

- Does the stem contain just one central theme? If not, can I reword it or split it into more than one item?

- Are the distractors plausible and do they make grammatical sense? Are any of the distractors clearly inappropriate?

- Is the correct answer clearly correct and up-to-date according to experts in the field?

If your test item satisfies all of these standards, it's a good one.

Design, Development, and Use of Performance Tests

Again, depending on the type of behavior you wish to measure, tests can be either written or performance-based.[2] Information and cognitive processing is best measured by written demonstration of knowledge. Measuring the learner's performance of the desired skills best tests motor skills ability. The processes, which I will describe here, will show you how to write content-valid performance tests (Cantor, 1988).

Like written test development, performance test development has three distinct phases: (1) designing the performance test; (2) preparing the test materials; and, (3) validating the test. Each phase has its own requirements, and when these are fulfilled, content validity is assured.

Designing the Test

Your first step is to create and record a test plan that specifies the particular performances to be tested. This process can be divided into three parts. First, define the specific purpose of the test. Second, analyze step-by-step the specific behaviors to be measured. Third, select the specific measurement points or scoring references (usually task elements or steps). Include

2Portions of this material originally appeared in J. A. Cantor, How to design, develop, and use performance tests. *Training and Development Journal*, 1988, September, 72-75.

approximate testing time. Together, these parts make up the design specification from which the test is written. This plan is a working document that should be completed, reviewed, and discussed early in the development process, and then revised as required to reflect the purposes of the performance test.

Test Plan: (1) Define the Purpose

Ideally, by first analyzing the purpose of the performance test and the behaviors to be measured, a determination of the best approach(es) for testing can be made. Constraints on administrative time or resources may dictate whether a *product* or *process* performance test is to be used. A product performance test requires the learner to actually produce an item or perform a series of tasks associated with the job from start to finish. A process performance test requires only a series of steps or tasks to be demonstrated. Any constraints or preferences regarding the testing method should be indicated in the test plan.

Most performance tests are either of a *pass/fail* nature, in which performance measurement is based on an established standard or criterion, or of a *normative* nature, in which the measurement of performance will compare each learner's skill mastery or competency with all other learners. Be sure to note an approximate test time and length in the test plan, as well as any constraints on the time available for testing. When deciding times, take into account the test purpose and subject matter to be covered.

Test Plan: (2) Analyze the Task

The test plan must indicate the performance-based behaviors to be tested. In order to identify the knowledge, skills, abilities, and tasks critical to carrying out the work associated with each subject area, it is necessary to analyze all appropriate instructional objectives in detail. This analysis is also an important part of establishing the content validity of the performance test.

The instructional objective review serves to identify:

- the specific behavioral elements that should be measured;
- whether a performance test or a written test is actually most appropriate for the measurement; and,
- the number of questions or trials needed to establish proficiency on a task or element.

Test Plan: (3) Select the Measurement Points

You may wish to ask several qualified subject matter experts to review and agree upon the critical measurement points (based on instructional objectives) to be used. Establish a process for recording relevant work and training experience of the people who are asked to judge test content. There are no specific guidelines on how much experience is enough, but they should have recent and relevant experience with the task being reviewed. Often a mix of people, including those who supervise the work as well as people who actually do the work, is best.

You should have each expert record which components of the task analysis data are important to the overall purpose of the test and which should be measured. The components include duties, tasks, task elements and knowledge, skills, and abilities. For example, if you want to measure a learner's performance on a specific task, such as overhauling a pressure valve, then tasks and task elements probably will be rated as more important to the end product, than to the analysis. If you want to measure overall job performance, then the knowledge, skills, and abilities will be rated higher. The level of detail in the analysis need only be deep enough to satisfy the intended purpose of the test. If you only, or one other person, such as another instructor, do the analysis of objectives and measurement selection, others actually working in the area should again review behavioral measurement points.

Decide how much time will be required to complete the test. Record all decisions in detail to make the specification clear. This process of definition and review is time consuming, but is necessary to ensure content validity. It also makes your job as the test writer much easier.

Preparing the Test Materials

Once the test has been designed select the testing materials needed to support learners in taking the test. Testing materials may include a proctor's (or supervisor's) guide, in addition to the performance test itself. Other materials may include directions, answer and information sheets, supporting documents, drawings, tools, machines, and other items needed during the test. Make a note of any task items or performance checkpoints that are governed or supported by documents, drawings, or directives. Write notes on the test item form or assessment checklist as appropriate. Also cite all matters of common industry practice. For instance, a technical standard might have an informational notation such as "all nuts are tightened to 57 foot-pounds."

Written directions should always accompany performance tests. A statement of purpose, procedures, materials, constraints, safety measures, and scoring methods is also important.

Figure 5-12 is an example of a performance assessment checklist.

Test Validity and Reliability

Before a test is used, it should be evaluated for validity and reliability (see Cantor, 1988; 1987a).

Validity is the extent to which a test measures what it claims to measure. Most competency-based tests should measure the cognitive-based knowledge, motor skills, and abilities required to function at a given level of competence in the job position. Tests that measure more or less than this are diminished in validity.

Example of a Performance Assessment Checklist

Name:_____   Badge No:_____   Code:_____

Trade: Machinist   Duty: Mills-Bridgeport

Title: Slotted Block   Check sheet, page 2 of 4 pages

Step	Check Points	Check Point Performance	Required Step Score	Maximum Possible Score	Actual Score	Step	
						Pass	Fail
D	Mill first and second surfaces	Totals	11	16			
	1. Select speed of cutter and feed of table.	SAT / UNSAT		1			
	2. Position end mill to right front of vise and mill side of block until clean.	SAT / UNSAT		5			
	3. Remove block and deburr.	SAT / UNSAT		2			
	4. Reinsert machined side against solid vise jaw, leaving about ½" extending beyond end of vice. Tighten and top down.	SAT / UNSAT		3			
	5. Mill second side until clean.	SAT / UNSAT		3			
	6. Deburr second side.	SAT / UNSAT		2			
	7. Dimensions (first two sides). First two sides milled are square ± .005".	SAT / UNSAT					
E	Mill second and third surfaces	Totals	9	11			
	1. Gauge sides one and two to ensure that they are square.	SAT / UNSAT		1			
	2. Insert a machined side against solid vise jaw. Tap down.	SAT / UNSAT		1			
	3. Mill third side to finished dimensions with O.D. micrometer.	SAT / UNSAT		3			
	4. Remove block and deburr.	SAT / UNSAT		1			
	5. Insert machined side against solid vise jaw and tap down.	SAT / UNSAT		1			
	6. Mill fourth side to finished dimension. Check dimensions with O.D. micrometer.	SAT / UNSAT		3			
	7. Remove block and deburr.	SAT / UNSAT		1			
	8. Dimensions (block length and width).	SAT / UNSAT					

Figure 5-12.

The test must reflect the competencies identified as critical in the job/task analysis, the instructional objectives, and the content specifications. That's why you review these documents at the outset of the test design process. Make sure you have a test item for each of the critical aspects of the job. Once you have arranged all your items into a complete test, it's a good idea to have other experts in the subject review your effort. They can tell you if you've missed anything. You should also administer the test to some competent job incumbents; their feedback will give you an idea of the test's real-world applicability.

While *validity* determines the degree to which a test measures what it claims to measure, *reliability* determines the degree to which it does so in a consistent manner. A written or performance test, like any other measuring instrument, is useless unless it can consistently produce reliable results.

Several factors influence a test's reliability. The most important is the appropriateness and technical accuracy of the test items. They must evaluate realistic and practical aspects of job performance. The number of test items is also important; the more test items, the better the ability of the test to measure competence. However, this is not a license for overkill: a three-step procedure probably doesn't warrant a 100-question test. Just make sure you test all the critical skills and knowledge adequately and completely. Objectives and associated test items should be analyzed separately.

Remember, too, that the order in which you present the items can affect test reliability. Just as improper distractors can cue the correct response, improper sequencing of items may give away answers. Make sure question one does not tip off the answer to question two. Also, make sure the correct answer to question two does not depend on knowing the correct answer to number one. Each item should present an independent problem.

You may not be able to control some of the factors affecting reliability, but you should be aware of them. Try to create a consistent atmosphere for test taking; uniformity of the examination environment is important. The same test administered once in a noisy and poorly lit factory area and again in a quiet classroom will probably yield very different results. Also realize that cheating will skew test results. You should arrange for as much test security and exam proctoring as is necessary.

Using a Computer to Develop Tests

Software programs are available to assist in developing tests and test items, and in administering exams and tracking student competencies. One such program has been developed by LXR-Test™ (see Figure 5-13). The LXR-Test™ software is an integrated testing package that runs on a Windows™ operating system platform. There are similar programs that run on a Macintosh ™ operating system.

Computer-based testing programs can perform many of the following functions:

- Accommodate many types of test items: multiple choice, true/false, matching, short-answer, open-ended, and numeric response.

  ☐ Depending upon the nature of the training program, and the particular inclinations of the instructor(s), testing may include any or all of these types of test items. A useful software program should be capable of supporting as many of the types of test items as the instructors wish to use.

- Accommodate an unlimited number of items in each bank.
- Select items based on any content or classification.

  ☐ The software design should be capable of supporting a bank of test items.

  ☐ An ability to develop multiple versions of the same test is often useful in some training programs. This

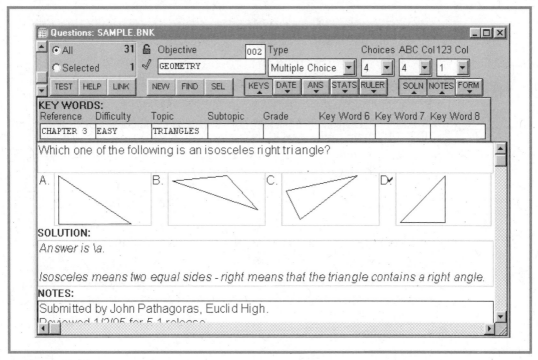

Figure 5-13.

permits instructors to ensure testing security where there are multiple numbers of a course running simultaneously.

☐ The software should allow the items, as developed, to be numerically coded to the corresponding performance objective that it tests. Data about an individual student's progress can then be directed to the student's performance record.

• Provide true word processing capabilities with text styling, rulers, and tabs.

☐ The software should have a built-in 100,000 word spelling checker.

☐ It should also support multiple color graphics and QuickTime™ movies.

☐ The program needs page layout capabilities and must permit moving graphics independently of text. It is essential that a software program have a true word processing capability. Instructors should be able to easily manipulate test, graphics, etc.

- Classify items by any testing objective and optionally by up to 8 separate keyword categories.
- Link reference material to dependent items.
- Store related instructions, graphics, and passages.

  ☐ Once test items are developed, the instructor should be able to build tests to support units of instruction or the entire course. Items must be keyed to objectives in the training program, and the software should have the capability to identify these items by objective coding. Likewise, any graphics or reference materials supporting the items should be codeable in the software.

- Track item statistics—including name and date of test where each item was last used.
- Finally, the software should support item response tracking for analysis purposes. Herein, the instructor can monitor lesson effectiveness, as well as student progress.

Summary

Validity and reliability determine the value of your test, but if you follow the general principles of test item writing you will be off to an excellent start.

Base your test items on the critical job-performance criteria identified in the program design documents. Choose a test item format that suits the nature and complexity of the central theme you want learners to recall. Develop test item stems so they focus on one central theme and provide learners with all the information necessary to answer the question. Create plausible distractors that make grammatical sense and write them so they follow the stem logically. Finally, be sure that your correct answer is really correct.

Remember that test item writing is an art, and just as painters must hone their skills, so must item writers. It may be an art, but it is an art that can be learned. Continued practice will make you a good test item writer, one whose tests measure critical skills, abilities, and understanding with validity and reliability.

Chapter References

Baird, M., et al. (1985). Training and the law: What you don't know might hurt. In *The training and development sourcebook*. Boston, MA: Human Resource Development Press.

Cantor, J. A. (1988, September). How to design, develop, and use performance tests. *Training and Development Journal*, 72-75.

Cantor, J. A. (1987a, May). Developing multiple-choice test items. *Training and Development Journal*, 85-88.

Cantor, J. A. (1987b). *The design of criterion-referenced tests to support vocational program evaluation*. Paper presented to the American Vocational Association, Las Vegas, NV.

Dick, W. W., & Carey, L. (1978). *The systematic design of instruction*. Glenview, IL: Scott, Foresman.

Driscoll, M. P. (1994). *Psychology of Learning for Instruction*. Needham Heights, MA: Allyn & Bacon.

6

Lesson Planning for Effective Instruction

Teach them what they need to know: Use a mutual problem-solving approach to assist your learners to gain knowledge that has application.

Rationale for Planning

Does an inexperienced instructor need a written lesson plan? You bet. Does an experienced instructor need a written lesson plan? Absolutely. Regardless of your experience or educational background, you need a blueprint for success. A good lesson plan guides you in your task of assisting learners to achieve the instructional objectives, and helps ensure classroom order. It enables you to remember what you might otherwise forget as you stand in front of a group. Thus, it leaves nothing to chance. A lesson plan helps you organize and administer class activities. It is your script for effective instructional communication.

If you have ever attended a class in which the instructor was unorganized or ill-prepared, you will understand the value of lesson planning. Without a lesson plan, your thoughts may appear disjointed, your learners may become confused, and important topics or parts of the lesson may be left out.

Alternatively, with a lesson plan, you can: (1) ensure that instructional objectives are met; (2) keep yourself organized and on topic; (3) cue yourself on methodology, references, media and/or activities, etc., which are to be used at various points in the lesson; and (4) keep within your scheduled time. Hence, lesson plans provide a framework into which to arrange the knowledge, skills, abilities, and/or attitudes to be imparted so that a systematic and logical order is achieved. Furthermore, lesson plans can be used over again by you, and possibly by other instructors. They also attest to the training that has been conducted and provide documentation recognized by courts of law, should your organization be involved in litigation (Baird et al., 1985). Also see Chapter 11.

Therefore, regardless of your level of education or experience, or whether you have taught the lesson before, you need a written plan for every lesson you teach.

Components of Lesson Plans

When organizing lesson plans, it is essential to have answers to the five Ws, those familiar questions of who, what, when, where, why (and how). All plans must include these essential components: *who* (target audience), *what* (organization of topics and content), *when* (time frames), *where* (class location), *why* (instructional objectives, including kinds of learning), and *how* (learner assignments, materials needed, media/methodologies, and instructor outline and notes).

Audience Analysis

Before you can begin to construct lesson plans or even complete writing your instructional objectives, you must identify your target audience through audience analysis—the process of gathering relevant information about your target audience. In asking "Who are they?" audience analysis provides the answers for the *who* part of the lesson plan. This analysis can then guide you in planning instructional objectives, and in deciding on levels of instruction, appropriate activities, and your approach to teaching topics. Thus, audience analysis can help ensure the overall success of the instruction.

Audience analysis identifies the people who will receive the training and provides vital information about their backgrounds. A needs assessment identifies the need for training, and an occupational analysis identifies the specific training required. However, these processes do not constitute a mandate to train all personnel in the organization. You must target the specific audience for whom the training applies.

While the actual information about the audience that you will need varies, depending on your instructional situation, components of the audience analysis generally include:

- academic factors, such as the audience's prior schooling and training;
- reading level;
- background in subject matter;
- special or advanced courses completed, relating to subject matter;
- personal and social factors, e.g. age;
- special talents, expectations and vocational aspirations, motivation and attitude toward subject matter, and learning styles; and,
- special learning needs.

Audience analysis information can be used to determine who should be trained. It might be decided to include learners who:

- are new to the job or task;
- have practical experience with the job or task but no formal training;
- have formal training with the job or task but need on-the-job application training; and/or
- have performed incorrectly on the job or task in real or simulated situations.

Once you know who needs to be trained, it is a good idea to have some description of specific learner characteristics that may be of relevance in planning. You know that your audience may be diverse. For example, formal education may range from seventh grade to college. Further variations may exist in age, physical capabilities, psychological traits, work experiences, job title and rank, and special skills. Identification of these characteristics will help you avoid errors in planning. For example, different training must be designed for (a) apprentices versus seasoned technicians; (b) those with minimal reading/writing skills versus college graduates; (c) new recruits versus managers with 15 years experience; and (d) those certified in the subject versus those who are not.

Thus, occupational (job and task) analysis and audience analysis should complement each other. Determining training requirements, planning for that training, and targeting it to your audience appropriately will ensure that you *"teach them what they need to know."*

Sequencing Objectives

Your instructional objectives, written in behavioral terms, and their careful sequencing provide material for the *"what"* portion of your lesson organization. *Terminal objectives* are those that describe the ultimate performances expected for a particular lesson or unit of instruction. Terminal objectives are necessary when a particular lesson is so complex that the information must be broken into smaller pieces, or *enabling objectives*. Enabling instructional objectives are therefore subordinate to terminal objectives and aim for performances that ultimately demonstrate the terminal performance objective.

What has to be done now before planning and developing instruction? (See Figure 4-1; Chapter 4.) First, the objectives must be selected and sequenced for the course, and then also for the lesson or unit.

Why and What to Sequence

Sequencing is the process whereby terminal and enabling objectives are organized to provide for the most effective arrangement of the teaching/learning activities (GPU Nuclear, 1986). Proper sequencing offers several definite advantages.

- Appropriate sequencing ensures that skills and knowledge are developed in an orderly and progressive manner.

- Sequencing prevents unnecessary repetition and duplication, and/or gaps and omissions in the instruction.

- It provides organization and certainty for your learner. If a course is presented in the right sequence (according to a learning hierarchy), your learner feels comfortable, has maximum control of the learning environment (via *use of executive strategies*), and is able to master the learning. Therefore, I suggest that proper sequencing helps to motivate your learner by providing a sense of direction and accomplishment.

Once the objectives are logically ordered, an instructional outline can be developed. This outline will provide a basis on which to plan individual lessons and select learning materials.

How to Sequence

Sometimes there is more than one appropriate way to sequence your instructional objectives. Other times the sequence is dictated by the need to teach some objectives before others. Lessons are often developed around common themes. Themes for lessons frequently become self-evident as you are sequencing the instructional objectives for the course. Lessons may be built around as few as two or three large terminal objectives or as many as one or two dozen smaller ones.

Sequencing also permits terminal and enabling instructional objectives to be arranged to provide for the most effective teaching/learning activities. Remember, as discussed in Chapter 4, you must consider the ultimate performances desired of the learner when making sequencing decisions. Ask yourself again:

- What must your learner do? Remember something or do something?
- Will your learner do something with or without aids?

The answers to these questions will have an effect on the sequence you design (Cantor, 1985, as furthered by King et al., 2001).

To properly sequence objectives, two questions must be answered:

- In what order will the objectives be taught/learned?
- How will the learning content for each objective be arranged?

In answering these questions, you will probably first think of how you will teach the instructional objectives. However, you should make every effort to think of your learner's needs and point of view. What is the best arrangement for learning the objective? The best method is the one that produces the desired results in the shortest time, with your learner retaining the knowledge or skill for the longest time. Try to create a scheme that is intentionally designed from your learner's "learning" point of view. There are three methods of sequencing objectives.

Job Performance Sequence

One method of sequencing, which applies to many courses, is job performance order. In this method, the procedures of a task, or task elements, are arranged in the same order as performed on the job. As you can see, this method matches your learner's activities very closely to the actual job requirements and makes the instruction more realistic. Also, it is much easier for your learner to transfer what is learned in the course of instruction to the job performance in the learner's environment. Whenever you are teaching specific procedures, you should try to sequence them in the order of the job performance.

Simple to Complex Cognitive Sequence

This method of sequencing presents a progression that promotes understanding and makes learning easier. Whenever possible, the instruction progresses from the known to the unknown, from easy to difficult, and from concrete to abstract. This psychologically ordered sequence is designed to begin with your learner's present abilities and to progress from that point. Here are some examples:

- Instruction begins with something your learner already knows and progresses to new knowledge (known to unknown).

- Instruction begins with a short, simple procedure and continues until your learner has mastered a complicated procedure (easy to difficult).

- Instruction begins with a simple actual example and continues until underlying rules and principles have been learned (concrete to abstract).

Logical Performance Sequence

Sometimes the content of instruction will fall into a logical pattern because of the combined elements of job performance and psychological order. For greater learning effectiveness, teaching/learning activities should normally proceed from known to unknown, simple to complex, easy to difficult, etc. Unfortunately, many teaching/learning activities do not lend themselves to that order. Thus, your sequence must be a logical combination of the elements of the job performance and the desired psychological order. For example, the performance procedures might be in operational sequence, with the supporting skills and knowledge arranged in cognitive sequence.

General Rules for Sequencing

In actual practice, all sequencing plans have a place in instructional development. The sequence used should depend on the nature of the task or knowledge being taught and the availability of resources. However, the following rules are helpful in determining a sequence (US Navy, 1976):

- Whenever possible, place easily learned objectives early in the sequence.
- Introduce concepts at the first point where the understanding of the concepts is necessary for performance. For example, component operation may be taught just before inspection procedures.
- Introduce a concept or skill into the course where it is to be used.
- Introduce instruction on prerequisite skills prior to the time where they must be combined with other skills or where they are to be applied.
- Teach procedural skills and knowledge in the same sequence as required in the work environment, keeping in mind the limitations of equipment and facilities.
- Provide for practice of skills and concepts in subjects where transfer of learning is difficult to attain.
- Place complex skills late in the sequence.

Examples of Sequencing Objectives

Many people have learned to drive a car. Figure 6-1 lists the objectives a driver education instructor might be required to place in sequence. Read through the list and ask yourself the following two questions (Dick & Carey, 1978):

- In what order will the objectives be taught/learned?
- How will the learning content for each objective be arranged?

The sequence developed in Figure 6-1 is only one of many possible schemes. It was accomplished by separating the necessary background knowledge and information from the actual manipulative skills. The majority of objectives were easily placed into either group; a few were more difficult to categorize and needed to be further analyzed. All instructional objectives marked with a single asterisk are grouped as

Example of a Sequenced List of Objectives

A. *Adjust rearview and sideview mirrors for proper vision.

B. *Operate the turn signal selector.

C. *Select proper gear.

D. **Start the car.

E. Drive a running car that has previously been parked adjacent to a street curb on a side street with no other cars or obstructions in front of it.

F. Perform a K-turn on a two-lane side street which is blocked off to any other traffic.

G. Perform a K-turn on a two-lane side street open to traffic in either direction.

H. *Discuss the relevant rules of the road as listed in the state/provincial driver's manual.

I. *Locate and discuss the purpose of the following:

- gas pedal
- brake pedal
- clutch pedal
- shift selector
- turn signal
- oil pressure indicator
- battery charge indicator
- engine temperature indicator
- windshield washer control
- defogger and heater
- emergency brake
- light beam switch
- high beam switch
- parking light switch
- oil level dip stick

J. *State the insurance and registration requirements for licensing a car in your state/province.

K. Parallel park the car into a space fifteen feet in length, which is adjacent to the curb and bounded by orange rubber cones three feet high.

L. *Discuss the inspection procedure good drivers should perform prior to starting a car (as listed in the National Underwriters guideline).

M. *Determine if an engine has the proper quantity of crank case oil for normal use as indicated by the owner's manual.

Figure 6-1.

background. Instructional objectives without an asterisk are motor skills associated directly with driving. A double asterisk indicates an objective that does not seem to fall directly into the two groups. This example shows one method of developing a matrix that lists objectives in the order in which they should be taught.

Scheduling Instruction

In constructing lesson plans, once the audience analysis (the "who" component) and the sequencing of objectives (the "what" component) are completed, the "when" and "where" components must be addressed. You must clearly specify the dates, times, and locations of instruction. Special consideration must also be given to coordinating and scheduling training with other departments and supervisors. Also decide what space and equipment is required and check with others to be sure that you can secure use of these resources when you need them. The lesson plan will specify the outcomes of these efforts—specifically, when training will take place, and where it will be held.

Organizing Instructional Content

A key component of writing your lesson plan is deciding *how* to organize its content. Content may be presented on the basis of relationship, (related ideas or activities), position (pros and cons), or structure. It may be arranged according to journalism's five W's (who, what, when, where, and why), in terms of cause and effect, to reflect from least to most, or by phase.

When you have determined your organizing principles, divide the content into three categories—must know, need to know, nice to know (if you intend to include non-essential information). Be sure you cover the "must know" and "need to know" information before spending too much time on the "nice to know."

Next fill in the details, i.e. the methodologies, media, materials needed, activities, time frames, etc. Remember that all of these must be tied to and support the program goals and instructional objectives. Ensure that your learner always takes something away from the class (e.g. steps of a process, reasons for doing something). When you are finished, review the lesson plan for consistency and flow, and to ensure that all necessary items have been addressed (Draves, 1984). To check yourself, show the plan to a peer for comments.

Writing Lesson Plans: A Four-Step Process

When writing lesson plans, it is helpful to know that they are usually formatted in four steps: (1) motivation; (2) presentation; (3) application; and, (4) evaluation. These steps will provide the framework for ensuring that the nine events of learning take place (see Chapter 2). The four steps provide the basis for a well-developed oral presentation, such as a lesson or speech.

Step 1: Motivation

This step is intended to create learner interest, curiosity, and attention and make it clear *why* this material must be learned. You must use techniques that relate to the instructional objectives of the lesson in order to stimulate your learner's desire to learn the material. Be creative in designing motivational techniques—they can be simple or very complex—however, they must be effective if the rest of the lesson is to succeed.

Advance Organizers

An advance organizer is defined as introductory material presented to learners at a much more general level than the material to be learned later (Ausubel, 1978; Walls et al., 1982). Advance organizers in written or oral form can help your learners understand where the new material fits into the overall scheme of things. Organizers also help learners relate the material that will be covered in the lesson to previously learned information (current knowledge). Advance organizers are considered part of the motivation of the lesson as they arouse expectations and often entice the learner to want to receive the new information.

For example:

> Today, we will be learning how to establish a booster tank source. This comes under the major topic called SUPPRESSION. The specific unit under SUPPRESSION is called *Deploying Personnel and Equipment*. One of the jobs within that unit is to *Provide water supply,* and a task under that is to *Establish a booster tank source*. That's where we begin today.

Such an advance organizer makes clear to learners the structure in which the material to be learned belongs. It acts as a sort of mental framework and provides "pigeonholes" into which new information may be placed. Research indicates that helping the learner organize information in this way, so that the overall structure is understood, improves learning and retention. In other words, show learners where the material they will learn fits into the rest of their course, and the job.

Step 2: Presentation

Here the new skills, concepts, and/or procedures are introduced to your learners. These can be presented in a lecture, or a demonstration, or both, depending on the subject matter. Always present material in a way that promotes easy understanding *(semantic encoding)* of new information by your learners. The key concept to remember is that the method must match the objective of the lesson (Cantor, 1988). If you are instructing a skills application, then your learners must see the application in action. Figure 6-2 presents a format for a lesson plan.

To plan and lay out your presentation you must develop a logical and easy-to-follow flow of ideas and concepts. To accomplish this you should understand the components of a lesson presentation.

The five main lesson presentation components are:

Example of a Lesson Plan Format

LESSON TITLE: Introduction to Strategy   DATE: February 20__   TIME: 50 minutes
OBJECTIVE(S): The firefighter shall list 8 steps of firefighter strategy, followed by an explanation of each, with 100% accuracy.
MATERIALS: Overhead projector, Extension Cord, Screen, Overhead 1.2 & 2 overlay, Chalkboard.

Clock Time	Main Points	Methods, Media, Notes
5 min.	**MOTIVATION**	
	• Identify and consider the steps of firefighter strategy. • Prioritize these strategies to fit each individual incident. GOAL: To have a well-thought-out plan that will ensure the most important item, rescue, will be addressed first in our operations	
20 min.	**PRESENTATION**	
	• Define the single-company response.	Interactive lecture
	Solicit definitions from the students. Try to develop a definition such as: *"A single-company response is any response where one company responds and operates on the scene for more than 3 to 5 minutes before the arrival of additional units."*	List on chalkboard

	• Present an analysis of a firefighter response strategy.
	    The analysis below is by Fire Chief Alan Brunacini of Phoenix, Arizona.
	    RESCUE: locate safely, protect, and remove fire victims.
	    FIRE CONTROL: mount an aggressive, well-placed and adequate fire attack.
	    PROPERTY CONSERVATION: keep property loss to a minimum.
	• Explain importance of understanding the analysis.
	    Each of the 8 steps of strategy must be considered at every fire encountered. Often, only a few steps present problems, but we must consider each one before dismissing it.
	    All 8 steps of strategy are contained in Brunacini's analysis. An understanding of these steps is necessary before simplifying them into the three categories.
		Overhead #2

20 min.	**APPLICATION**	
	• Have each firefighter randomly select a single step and discuss its applications to fireground operations.	Recitation in front of class
5 min.	**EVALUATION**	
	• Each firefighter will list and explain verbally the 8 steps of firefighter strategy.	Verbally to instructor

Figure 6-2.

(1) A *statement* presents essential information needed by your learner to master the objective. For example, when teaching the parts of a lathe with the objective of remembering their names, a statement could be as simple as naming the lathe parts while the class watches a diagram or the actual equipment. Or learners might examine a labeled diagram contained in a "Learner's Guide." For an instructional objective that requires your learner to know how to prepare a message for transmittal, an oral statement or visual presentation of each step can be made to the class.

(2) *Practice remembering* provides an opportunity for your learners to test their ability by recalling or recognizing specific information presented in the statement. Some examples are: an oral quiz on the parts of a lathe or the steps for transmitting a message conducted during the presentation, written practice during class, or practice questions in the learner guide to be done as homework.

(3) A *task demonstration* physically demonstrates to your learners either in the classroom or the laboratory how to operate a lathe or how to transmit a message; alternatively, your learners could view slides, movies, videotapes, videodiscs, etc., that show how to do the task.

(4) Through *practice using* your learner is given an opportunity to perform the task. For example, your learners could be given a project to complete during which they would operate a lathe or transmit a message. For tasks where cost and safety must be considered, simulators could/should be used to provide practice using.

(5) *Feedback,* in conjunction with practice, should be given on the correctness of the answer or the quality of the performance. After practice remembering information (such as names of lathe parts or steps for message transmittal) that occurs in the classroom or is done as homework, you should review each question given and provide the correct answer. After practice doing tasks in the classroom or laboratory, you

should give either oral feedback or written evaluation. Different combinations of these components are required depending on the task level of the objective.

Flowcharts

Of paramount importance in the development of any lesson is the sequencing of the information for presentation. The information must be presented logically so that the learner can understand the relationships of ideas, concepts, and skills. Additionally, skills must be presented sequentially, usually from easy to difficult, for practice and reinforcement (see Chapter 4).

One way to make decisions about presentation order is by flowcharting. A flowchart is used to demonstrate visually a sequence of decisions and things to do (responses) based on those decisions. For example, computer programmers use flowcharts to illustrate the decisions and responses in a computer program.

For example, a statement in the program might say, "If A > B then go to 300." So, when the program is run and reaches that statement, if the value of variable A is greater than the value of variable B, the program skips to line 300.

Other fields besides computer science (e.g. the military, businesses, education) use flowcharts. Any strategy or series of steps (responses) may be arranged on a flowchart. Figure 6-3 presents a branching task analysis flowchart.

Step 3: Application

The application step provides an opportunity for your learners to test, practice, and reinforce the skills and information presented to them in the lesson, and so directly involves them in the learning process. This promotes rehearsal of information to ensure that it is maintained in short-term memory and finally encoded for storage in long-term memory. Performance in the actual environment is preferable. All lessons must provide for an

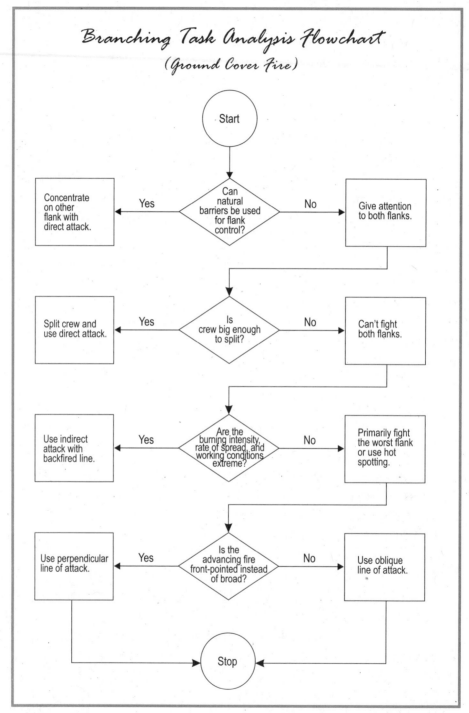

Branching Task Analysis Flowchart
(Ground Cover Fire)

Figure 6-3.

application of information, whether physical skills or cognitive processes are involved.

Step 4: Evaluation

Evaluation tools test both learner performance and information/skill acquisition, and your effectiveness as an instructor. Evaluation of learners can be as simple as a verbal check (asking questions of your learners) or as complex as a written and/or performance examination (described in Chapters 5 and 9).

When you finish teaching a course, like many instructors you may feel a mixture of relief, elation, sadness, and regret. There is relief that it is over. The constant tension of being the leader, trying to communicate, getting your learners to learn, and handling all the big and little details is over. Regardless of how much instructors like to teach, they feel relief. When your evaluations are good, you feel good. When your learners come up and shake your hand and tell you what a great instructor you are and what a valuable course it was, you are pleased.

However, most instructors are disappointed at written evaluations that question their teaching ability in even a minor way.

> I wonder what I did to make this person rate me as only average on answering questions completely?

> Gee whiz, a couple of people only gave me a 4 instead of a 5 on knowing the subject thoroughly.

> I bet I know why a few people marked the item down a little—talk about tolerating differences of opinion. It was probably when I disagreed with Sandy.

> Oh no, look at this comment. It says I should try to be a little more organized.

Even the most experienced instructors feel a pang. Many have given up looking at evaluations because they are painful. Failure is difficult to face; it does not have to be a major blunder to be considered disturbing. As instructors, we are a sensitive and caring group. We want to be effective in facilitating learning, changing behaviors, and reducing performance discrepancies for our learners. We realize that there is no absolutely perfect instructor. We want to do better in the areas in which others perceive us to be less than perfect. How should we go about this?

The 1-Thing Rule

A very useful concept to know and remember at this point is the "1-Thing Rule." Suppose you have a learner who has several problems: makes socially inappropriate comments in class, fails the test on electronics, is having trouble in the present unit, has a running interpersonal feud with another learner, is sloppy, and has other difficulties as well. How do you help? You cannot completely overhaul this person. You can only work with specific behaviors. You should concentrate on one problem at a time. Work with the one behavior that is most troublesome or the one in which you think you can make a difference.

What does this story about a learner with a lot of problems have to do with using feedback from evaluations to improve teaching? The same principle applies. If you try to improve several things at once, you probably will not change much in any area. Use the "1-Thing Rule," which means work on one thing at a time. Take first things first, one at a time.

- Pick either the item from the evaluation that troubles you the most or the one on which you think you can make most headway.
- Define the behavior so you know what it is.
- Decide what you are going to do differently the next time you teach.
- Do it.

A Final Word

If instructors have only surface understanding of the four "steps" of a lesson plan (motivation, presentation, application, evaluation) discussed in the preceding sections, they will have an oversimplified view of the lesson planning process. Motivation is not something you step into and then leave as you move to the next step. Presentation and application should alternate back and forth. You can have a 2-minute presentation, then a 1-minute application, followed by a 15-minute presentation, and a 5-minute application, then a 10-minute presentation, and then finally a 45-minute application. Summary can occur at various times. All lesson plans must have an evaluation component, which can be carried out at intervals throughout the instructional process, as well as at the end. Although the four steps must be understood clearly in order to plan effectively, in practice they should always be interwoven into the fabric of instruction.

Summary

Instructors should never blindly follow the four steps of a lesson plan. How many times have you looked at a lesson plan handed to you to use and thought something like, "Boy, this is going to be boring." Never slavishly follow a dry and deadly lesson plan. Certainly, you must present the content. Do not compromise the integrity of the subject matter. You owe it to yourself and your learners, however, to adapt the lesson plan, as necessary, to breathe life into it. Design a couple of activities, problems, or discussions to vary the lesson and keep a lively pace. Motivate your learners and do not let them get away. Sum things up and test when necessary. Retain the lesson, but adapt the plan to suit you and your learners.

Additionally:
- Involve your learners as much as possible; make them accountable for achieving objectives.
- Create a learning environment that will be effective for the lesson (Chapter 11).
- Ensure that the lesson plan supports the instructional objectives.
- Use a technical writing style in your lesson plans.

- Don't over-structure a lesson (e.g. provide too many facts or schedule every minute of class); allocate time realistically.

- Be sure that content is accurate. Provide handouts and further references when appropriate.

- Use a variety of teaching methods (Chapter 7).

- Adapt lessons to your teaching style.

- Rotate through the four steps of a lesson (motivation, presentation, application, evaluation) as needed. Do not be afraid to alternate between these steps throughout a lesson.

- Do not lecture for more than 20 to 30 minutes before including an application or activity.

- Use media that support the instructional objectives (Chapter 11).

Chapter References

Ausubel, D. P. (1978). "In defense of advance organizers: A reply to critics." *Review of Educational Research, 48,* 251-257.

Baird, M., et al. (1985). "Training and the law: What you don't know might hurt." In *The Training and Development Sourcebook.* Boston, MA: Human Resource Development Press.

Cantor, J. A. (1985). Task evaluation: Comparing existing curricula to task analysis results. *Journal of Educational Technology Systems, 14* (2), 157-163.

Cantor, J.A. (1988). The training effectiveness algorithm. *Journal of Educational Technology Systems, 16* (3), 207-229.

Dick, W. W., & Carey, L. (1978). *The systematic design of instruction.* Glenview, Ill: Scott, Foresman.

Draves, W. K. (1984). *How to teach adults.* Manhattan, KS: The Learning Resources Network.

GPU Nuclear Corp. (1986). *Training for performance: Basic instructor course text,* Parsippany, NJ: Educational Development Section; Training and Education Department, unpublished.

King, S. B., King, M., Rothwell, W. J. (2001). *The complete guide to training delivery: A competency-based approach.* New York: American Management Association.

National Fire Academy (NFA undated). Module #23: Build for the future with your course report. In *Student manual: Principles of instruction*. Emmitsburg, MD: Author, unpublished.

United States Department of the Navy. (1976). *Training specifications manual (Naval Air Maintenance Training Group)*. Washington, DC: I-6-16.

Walls, R. T., Haught, P. A., & Dowler D. L. (1982). *How to train new skills: Planning, teaching, evaluating*. Dunbar, WV: Research and Training Center Press.

7

Methods of Instructional Delivery

Not all learning comes from books: use your learners'
experiences to help teach.

Instructional methods are the various approaches, strategies, and procedures by which you convey knowledge, information, skills, etc., to your learners. Training will be most effective if you choose carefully those methods most suited to the instructional objectives. It is also more effective if you vary the method(s) used during each training session. Therefore, it is your responsibility first to evaluate your objectives and then to select a set of methods and activities that will match your instructional needs. This will result in more meaningful learning experiences for your learners.

The ultimate goal is to ensure that the method of instruction is experience-centered to maximize the use of your learner's past experiences and thus facilitate mastery of new information. This is best achieved when you remember that your role as an instructor is to be *leader, helper, guide, change agent, coordinator,* and *facilitator of learning.*

In practice, you must consider many factors when selecting (an) instructional method(s), including:

- the instructional content, to determine which methods are best suited for the material;
- your learner's needs, including motivation, background, levels of knowledge/skill, and preferences for a particular instructional method.

Your choice of method must complement the kind of learning to be undertaken by your learner. There are many different training methods, many different conditions under which training is presented, and many different kinds of training media. When preparing to instruct, keep these factors in mind and use the best method for a given set of circumstances.

This chapter discusses (1) instructional methods and how they correlate with the different types of training objectives; and (2) how you, as the instructor, must interact with your learner and the course material.

Methods of Instruction

Rarely does only one instructional method work for all learners or provide them with sufficient learning experiences. Nor is one particular instructional method suitable in all training situations. You should try to use several different methods of instruction in a single training session. Select the best instructional method for each segment of the required learning as indicated by the instructional objectives. Provide variety for your learners—this helps to hold their attention and maintain their interest. It also meets different learning style needs.

There are numerous methods of instruction. The more popular methods fall into three categories: (1) classroom instruction, including lecture, guided discussion, case-study, and role-playing; (2) laboratory experiences, including demonstration and simulation; and, (3) on-the-job training, including in-plant tours, one-on-one skills training, and apprenticeships.

Classroom Instruction

Lecture Method

The lecture, the traditional classroom mode of instruction, usually refers to a formal presentation of information, concepts, or principles by a single individual, such as you, the instructor. A lecture can be formal or informal and can be modified to include discussion, demonstration, and application. The formal lecture is usually a technique used before large groups with no active participation required of learners. This makes the learning experience passive. With little or no learner participation, much information tends to be lost during the lecture. This method is also inappropriate for skill training.

The informal lecture is appropriate for a smaller group and can be designed to encourage active learner participation, through a three-way exchange of comments, questions, and answers, involving the instructor, the learner, and the class (see Chapter 3).

Although the lecture method is passive (learners are not actively involved), it offers several advantages.

- Lecturing is a convenient method for instructing large groups. If necessary, a public address system can be used to ensure that all learners can hear.

- It permits the presentation of many ideas in a short time. Material that has been logically organized to facilitate selective perception on the part of your learners can be presented concisely and rapidly.

- The lecture is particularly suitable for introducing a subject or presenting basic information. It ensures that all learners have the necessary background to learn subsequent advanced subject material at a later time.

- A lecture is useful when giving directions for an activity or for summarizing the main points developed in discussions elsewhere.

The lecture method also has limitations and disadvantages, as outlined below.

- Lecturing is not appropriate for certain types of learning, e.g. acquiring manipulative skills. Learners can only develop such skills through practice.

Figure 7-1.

- Lecturers tend to present too much information in a short period of time. The passive listener does not retain much of this information.

- Learning is an active process, but the lecture method tends to foster passivity and dependence on the part of the learner. Learners do not feel adequately involved and responsible for their learning. Remember, adult learners need to be involved (see Figure 7-1).

- Feedback is limited, especially in formal lectures. Instructors lack adequate means of determining what has been learned and may not be able to estimate a learner's progress.

Holding question and answer periods frequently during the lecture can minimize some of these limitations. Also, to increase effectiveness, lectures should always be supported with ample visual aids such as whiteboards, flipcharts, handouts, slides, and PowerPoint and overhead projections (see Chapter 10 for instructional media). Videotaping the lecture further extends its usefulness. It is probably the easiest instructional method to videotape, as there is only one presenter who is generally stationary. A videotaped lecture can be used later either for individualized instruction or for small group presentations. Videotaping also allows you to observe how you come across to the audience.

Techniques for a Successful Lecture

Analyze

To prepare for a successful lecture, you must first analyze your audience (described in Chapter 6 on lesson planning). Knowing the general technical and educational background of your learners and their past experience will help you choose the best instructional organization and media for the material to be presented. Possibly another instructor, or someone who has previously worked with the group of learners, may be able to tell you what to expect.

Organize

Now, determine the purpose of the lecture, and then organize it by choosing the main points and arranging them in logical order. Whenever the lecture will evolve into a discussion, avoid covering the points yourself that the learners are to develop during the discussion.

Initiate

Consider the first 30 minutes of the lecture. The very first moments often set the pace for the lesson—use them wisely. It is usually a poor technique to launch into a lecture without some interaction with the audience. Get all learners involved actively as early as possible and keep them involved as often and as much as you can. Ricks (1982) and Walls in NFA (undated) suggest that during the first 30 minutes, everyone should make direct eye contact with at least a half dozen or so other learners. This begins the formation of a class community or learner-centered environment, per McClure et al. (2003).

Guided Discussion Method

The guided discussion method is an instructor-controlled, interactive process of meeting instructional objectives by sharing information and learner experiences in the classroom. In a guided discussion, you ask focused questions and periodically summarize concepts and principles covered, but you do not to dominate the discussion. Unlike the lecture, in a guided discussion your learners are more active participants. They are encouraged to explore a subject by actively offering knowledge, ideas, opinions, and experiences. They are often reassured that others share similar feelings and problems. The flow of communication is among all of your learners and you, rather than just between individual learners and you. A guided discussion can follow a lecture. As the instructor, you will frequently present information and then launch a discussion on a few key points. *Remember, your goal is to be a facilitator, guide, leader, and change agent.*

The discussion method can serve several purposes.

- Through discussion a deeper understanding of topics on which there are different points of view is achieved.

- It provides learners with opportunities to improve skills in reasoning and problem solving.

- This method leads to the development of knowledge and encourages changing attitudes (useful in supervisory, management, or safety training).

- "Refresher" knowledge and concepts can be provided through discussion in such areas as re-qualification training when the purpose is to review material.

A guided discussion has several limitations.

- The size of the group limits the use of a guided discussion (a group of 5 to 10 works well).

- You must be willing to give up some of your control of the training session. You cannot simply present the material directly to your learners yourself. Often, you start the process by posing an introductory leading question. Then, you, as an instructor, must carefully follow the discussion and direct proceedings only when and if necessary. You must not lose patience with your learners and, at the end of the session, be able to summarize points made.

- Learners must have sufficient confidence in you as the discussion leader to talk and question freely. They must be able to raise a controversial or unpopular point of view. Reticent learners may find this method difficult or intimidating.

- A guided discussion requires as much preparation time as a lecture, but takes more time as a training activity. Generally, more time is necessary to cover a topic through guided discussion than with a lecture or a film.

Techniques for a Successful Guided Discussion

Plan

First, you must determine the basic purpose of the discussion. Summarize what you want to convey about the subject. Devise and list a few questions to start the discussion and get major points across. However, these questions should not prevent the discussion from flowing naturally. The learners may need to complete a reading or other assignment beforehand. Determine whether visual materials will help the discussion, and, if so, prepare and use them. A pertinent video may generate interest, focus on the point to be discussed, or provide learners with needed background material. Provide some equipment, such as a whiteboard or a flipchart and felt-tip marking pens, for listing the important points to be made during the discussion, as well as questions left unresolved. You should do the writing. This will provide an orderly, complete record to summarize the discussion, and later help evaluate the training event.

If the classroom permits, plan an informal seating arrangement, such as a circle or horseshoe (see Chapter 11), so that your learners can easily see each other and the class or training leader. This arrangement helps generate discussion.

Initiate

Clarify the topic to be discussed and arouse interest in it *(develop appropriate expectancies for learner selective perception)*. A brief lecture, a motion picture, an amusing story, a short description of an actual situation, or perhaps a reference to an assignment the learners have just completed all provide an interesting basis for opening the discussion. Materials, such as a series of case problems, questions, and factual data, can also stimulate meaningful discussion about certain topics.

Phrase your questions to require more than just a "yes" or "no" answer. At the same time, make the questions concrete enough to permit your learners to organize their thinking and respond within a few minutes. Rather than simply asking, "What is supervision?" ask, "What characteristics have you noticed in good supervisors you have known?" Be prepared to wait for someone to respond. It requires courage to last through those moments of silence while your learners think about the topic and decide what they wish to say. They may be reluctant to speak, because they feel that they have nothing important enough to say or that others can say it better. As a last resort, you may need to call on an outgoing individual to get the discussion started.

Guide

Encourage your learners to do most of the talking until you have an idea of how much they know and where you, as the resource person, can best make your contribution. Ensure that each learner who wishes to speak gets the opportunity to do so. Shy learners, whose facial expressions indicate they are almost ready to speak, should be encouraged by a smile or a nod, but never forced to participate. No one should be allowed to dominate the discussion; learners who tend to do so may be tactfully discouraged by a remark such as: "While we're on this point, let's hear how some of the others feel about it," or "Could we save your other points until later and come back to them if we have time?"

Repeat some of your learners' ideas in order to emphasize the vital points that have been made. When necessary, offer information, correct misunderstandings, and bring out additional points of view. In doing so, make your comments brief and to the point. Draw the learner back into the discussion.

Keep the discussion on the subject. Not only do learners expect this of the instructor, but they also maintain greater interest in a discussion that has direction than in one that rambles. One way to get back on course is to summarize briefly what has been said up to that point. Then ask questions to encourage learners to go on from there.

Promote an exchange of opinions among learners. Encourage them to use the comments of others, as well as their own, in the discussion. "The following points have just been made. How do these influence the conclusions we reached earlier?" When a prolonged silence occurs, find out its cause by using open-ended questions. By watching body movements and facial reactions, you can usually tell whether your learners are bored, confused, in agreement, or in disagreement. If your learners appear confused, summarize what has been covered up to that moment, encouraging questions. If disagreements arise, try by your own calm behavior to gain respectful, good-humored attention for all points of view. You should not become emotionally involved in the argument itself.

End

Watch for signs of restlessness and end the discussion while interest is still high. If appropriate, summarize the major points that have been made or have a learner summarize them. If major points have not been adequately covered in the discussion, include these in your summary. You may find that learners will linger after class to talk about their ideas. Some may have been too shy to speak in class, but have excellent comments to make. Encourage them to share ideas with the group at the next opportunity. If interest is keen, encourage your learners to continue the discussion among themselves after class.

Case-Study Method

The case-study method uses a detailed written description of a real or imaginary situation that can be analyzed and discussed by your learners. A case study may describe a labor or personnel problem, operating problem, or incident appropriate to training. It can deal with the behavior of a person or a group. Presenting a case study enables your learner to develop skills by responding to various situations. It gives learners an opportunity to apply new knowledge. It stimulates discussion and participation.

Case studies are particularly useful in helping learners explore different ways to deal with typical problems in the workplace. However, the case must be well prepared and focused on a similar problem area. Cases are usually designed to focus on only one or two aspects of a situation, and the facts presented in the case descriptions tend to relate to these aspects alone. This method is appropriate for supervisory, clerical, and safety training. In fact, the case study method has become very popular in recent years for homeland security training.

Techniques for Successful Case Studies

Present

Choose a problem or case study that involves decision and action. It should offer complex problems that lack obvious solutions.

State the problem or case study briefly and simply. It can be made believable by including actual statements of individuals involved in the problem. These will be used to reveal attitudes and feelings. Distribute a copy of the case study to each individual, referring to it when necessary.

Include definite instructions explaining exactly what is to be done. These instructions are usually in the form of questions, either oral or written, asking how to solve the problem.

Solve

Give individual learners time to work on the problem and arrive at a solution. Conduct a discussion to help the individuals use problem-solving techniques. Guide your learners to consider each of the following steps:

- Identify the real problem. Looking for answers to questions such as who, what, when, where, and why will help you pinpoint the problem and its causes.
- Gather all the facts; eliminate guesswork and opinions.
- Evaluate the facts.
- Develop possible solutions.
- Select the best solution and apply it.
- Evaluate the results and readjust as necessary.

Although all steps may not apply to a particular problem or case study, learners should be aware of them.

In summary, case studies are used to allow your learners to test their conceptions, procedures, and practices in work-like situations. They help increase your learners' powers of observation, abilities to analyze, and problem-solving talents. They cause your learners to translate vague principles and practices into practical what-to-do's and how-to-do's. This method is one of the best ways to train individuals how to think.

Role-Playing Method

In role-playing your learners act out a situation based on real life. No acting ability is necessary because of the real-life quality of the situation. Learners role-play the attitudes and behaviors involved in carrying out a task or job responsibility. For example, your learners may be asked to assume roles such as "the overly enthusiastic secretary," "the bossy supervisor," or "the worker unconcerned with safety." The outcome of the activity depends upon the behavior spontaneously arising from these attitudes and emotions. In most role-playing, real feelings develop.

There are numerous benefits derived from role-playing.

- It is a highly participatory activity as each learner assumes a role and acts out an attitude or situation relevant to the job.
- It is useful in improving skills involved in working with people.
- It helps learners become aware of the reasons behind the behavior and the effect of their own behavior on others. This awareness causes the role-players and observers to more closely experience the feeling and reactions connected with the situation.
- It provides a more vivid experience than merely talking about a problem.
- It lends reality to any theory that has been presented.

Role-playing also has limitations.

- It must be restricted to clear-cut problems and situations.
- Role-playing requires careful supervision and direction by you, the instructor.
- There is always the possibility that emotions will be so intensely evoked and vividly portrayed as to disturb the players or the audience.
- Learners may experience anxiety in anticipation of having to play a role.
- It takes a great deal of training time.

Techniques for Successful Role-Playing

Select

Choose a meaningful situation for your learners. However, the first time role-playing is to be carried out, choose a situation that does not directly include the specific job responsibilities of any of the learners. They will be able to observe and analyze more objectively a situation that does not "hit too close to home." In the discussion following the role-playing, you can help your learners relate what they have observed to their own jobs.

Dramatize

Let your learners volunteer for the activity rather than suggesting that they take parts. Give instructions to each player, clearly detailing whom that player is and how that player "feels" at the beginning of the acting. Point out to the players that they must discipline themselves to react to the behavior of others, not as they normally would, but as would the people they are supposed to be. Give them a few minutes of privacy to get into the mood of their roles.

During this time, describe the situation to the rest of the class; you may or may not inform them of the specific emotions to be portrayed. They should play the role of objective observers. Give them clear instructions as to what they should be looking for. Allow the role-playing to continue until real feelings develop among the players. This usually takes from three to seven minutes of action. The purpose of this activity is to stimulate appreciation of the human behavior involved in the situation. It is not necessary to continue the action until the situation is resolved.

Discuss

After the role-playing, discuss what occurred. Your aim should be to help your learners increase their knowledge, skills, or attitudes based upon the experience. Start the discussion by having the players tell why they behaved as they did and describe what their inner responses were to the behavior of the others in the situation. This allows the players to set the tone of the criticism. For example, if the players show, by their own observations, that they are not self-conscious, all observers are more likely to feel free to express their full reactions.

The discussion may be developed along the lines of questions such as these: Did any player suddenly change behavior? Why do you think this happened? As time went on, did the players seem to understand each other, more or less? Why? How do you think the action would have ended, had it continued? What might the players have done to improve their relationship?

At first you should keep your learners focused on the role-playing. Then you should help your learners relate the analysis to their jobs, but keep specific names out of the discussion.

Laboratory Experiences

Demonstration Method

The demonstration method is a basic instructional process that can be used to teach motor skills. This method begins with a practical step-by-step performance by the instructor of a process, procedure, or other activity, with a detailed explanation accompanying each step. A demonstration should be accompanied or immediately followed by having learners practice the activity or skill being demonstrated for reinforcement and appropriate *semantic encoding* into long-term memory.

A demonstration has several advantages.
- It is especially helpful in technical and skill training, providing the link between explanation and practice.
- Demonstration, accompanied by learner practice, is an excellent method for teaching learners how to perform activities that require attention to detail and a high degree of accuracy. Completing time sheets or manipulating the control room console are examples of this type of activity.
- By watching a demonstration, listening to you explain what you are doing, and then performing the activity themselves, your learners are more likely to encode the

skill and information into working memory than if they simply heard an explanation or watched a demonstration.

- Actual practice also offers your learners the opportunity to be physically active after periods of passive sitting and listening.

Unless a demonstration is done properly, it will be of limited value. A good demonstration requires a great deal of preparation time. A demonstration should use the actual equipment or materials learners will work with on the job.

The only way to master a skill is by doing—not by seeing. A demonstration of a skill to be imitated by your learner should not last too long. The group must be small enough so that all learners will be able to see and hear the demonstration clearly. Class time must be sufficient for all steps of the demonstration. Some demonstrations suffer from too rapid a presentation. Avoid presenting something new before the preceding point is assimilated. People can only master one thing at a time.

Techniques for A Successful Demonstration

Plan

First, break down the activity or skill into logically ordered steps. Decide whether your learners should practice each step immediately after you demonstrate it or not until you have finished the entire demonstration and explanation. Allow sufficient class time for an introduction, step-by-step demonstration and explanation, thorough practice by your learners with guidance by you, and final discussion and review. Arrange the training area so that all learners can clearly see and hear the demonstration. Have the necessary materials in order and within easy reach.

Present

Describe what you are going to demonstrate, explain its value to your learners (to develop *appropriate expectancies*), and alert your learners to what in particular they should watch for (formulate *selective perception*). Show and explain the activity or skill, or the steps of it, one at a time. Answer questions and perform a step again if necessary. Have your learners try what you have demonstrated either after each step or at the end of your demonstration (*promote rehearsal*). Allow sufficient practice time so that all of your learners may receive guidance. Encourage your learners who already know the skill, or learn it quickly, to help others. At the end of the practice time, emphasize again how learners may use the new activity or skill on their jobs. Review the steps demonstrated. Describe the equipment needed and suggest possible substitutes. Suggest resources for further study.

Four-Step Skill Training Method

The four-step skill training method is an extension of the demonstration method and can be used to teach any motor (manipulative) skills. To prepare for a training session, there are certain steps which you, as the instructor, must take to ensure effective learning. The four steps described below should be followed when preparing for motor skills instruction.

The Preparation Step

Preparation of your learner includes those things you can do to better prepare a learner to receive the information. For example, state the instructional objectives at the beginning of a training session to ensure *selective perception*. This preparation step is the motivation portion of the lesson and should be included in motor skills training as well as cognitive instruction.

The Presentation Step

This step includes presenting the new subject material to the learner(s) in the form of both cognitive information and/or motor skills procedures. It is done in one or both of the following ways:

- explanation by lecture or guided discussion; and/or,

- demonstration telling what to do, showing how to do it, and then offering an opportunity to do it.

Remember to teach complicated skills in parts. As your learners master each part, move to the next part.

The Application Step

During this step, your learners actually apply or put into practice what has been explained or demonstrated to them. They "learn by doing."

As an instructor, you must lead your learners to think, talk, write, and act. This can be accomplished by using guided discussion, demonstration, or practice methods. Be sure to supervise the learning situation closely and stay available to answer questions that may arise. Have your learner explain what steps or tasks are involved in performing a task. Quickly correct any mistakes in either learner performance or explanation.

The Evaluation Step

Here is where you find the answer to the question "Did your learners learn?" Until this question is answered, neither you nor your learners can know how effective the training session was. The primary purpose of evaluation is *not,* as many instructors (and learners) think, to provide a means of rating or grading performance. The primary purpose is to provide information to the learner about the areas of the instruction in which there is weakness. It also provides you with information about which parts of the training were successful and which parts need revision.

Examinations are not only done at the end of a training session. Good instruction involves continual evaluation during all steps of instruction. Examine and correct the learner as learning occurs. The specific purpose of the examination and the type of learning covered will largely determine which type of test you should use. As was discussed in Chapter 5, a performance test, not a written test, should be used to examine manipulative skills.

The Follow-Up Step

This is an informal fifth step in the four-step method of instruction. In skills training, this step involves a later evaluation of on-the-job practices to determine if skills learned during training are actually being used or are being used correctly. If they are not being used at all, do not jump to the conclusion that the training was ineffective. Many times, skills are not used due to factors unrelated to training. This situation requires careful analysis before retraining or more training is prescribed. If these skills are being used, but incorrectly, chances are that the learning was not complete.

Simulation Method

Simulation is one of the most important and effective methods of instruction in many fields. By using simulators (a mock-up or duplicate of equipment, controls, etc.) your learners are able to practice skills in a controlled environment without constant anxiety over making mistakes that will endanger themselves, others, or the equipment. This makes it a "safe" training experience, which is especially important for operator training in highly complex and automated industries.

Simulators are computer-controlled devices that are programmed to coordinate graphic and auditory stimuli in an interactive enactment of a work situation or environment. Your learner reacts to information presented by the simulator that, in turn, simulates the same kind of reaction that would happen should that skill or information demonstration be offered in the "real-time" work environment.

Simulators are expensive pieces of equipment. Not all firms or organizations can afford them. One example of simulation is the replica simulator found at some nuclear power facilities. This machine electronically reproduces actions of a nuclear control room. If such apparatus is available, use it wisely. Practice on the simulator must be preceded by necessary lower level learning of motor skills and knowledge. In all simulation activities, initial practice sessions should be kept short and gradually lengthened as your learners' abilities improve.

On-The-Job Training

On-the-job training (OJT) is formal training that uses the workplace as the focal point for instruction. OJT should be planned and based on specific instructional objectives and evaluated for effectiveness through learner follow-up on the job. OJT provides a real opportunity to improve employee performance and satisfaction and, ultimately, to improve the efforts of the entire work force at minimal cost to the organization.

There are several kinds of on-the-job training, including the in-plant tour, one-on-one skills training, and apprenticeship. All involve the transmitting of well-defined job skills from a master technician, craftsman, artisan, manager, or other kind of knowledgeable employee, to another employee—your learner. The OJT instructor (the master) is sometimes the learner's supervisor or another skilled employee designated by the supervisor or by you.

On-the-job training is best conducted in your learners' own regular workplace and should always begin with an orientation to the workplace. This is often provided through an in-plant tour, a technique also used in conjunction with other forms of formal training.

In-Plant Tour

The in-plant tour is one of the most effective ways to familiarize learners with the work environment. It may or may not be used with on-the-job training. When used in conjunction with lectures, the in-plant tour reinforces knowledge of plant layouts and systems. During the tour, your learners should be encouraged to ask questions, as the flow of communication should be among all learners and you, rather than between individual learners and you. You must carefully construct the lecture and in-plant tour to ensure consistency and attain the desired outcomes. The in-plant tour method has several advantages.

- Tours actively involve your learners with the work environment and equipment.
- A tour can reduce fear of the plant and equipment.
- It appeals to several senses (see, hear, touch, smell).
- This method creates interest and reinforces learning.

The in-plant tour method also has limitations.

- A tour may be impossible because of plant or systems conditions.
- Special safety precautions must be observed.
- Small class size is required.
- Noise and other distractions compete for the learner's attention.
- The procedure is time-consuming.

Techniques for a Successful In-Plant Tour

Plan

Before the tour, clearly define its goals. Then plan the tour route and ensure site accessibility. Plant operations personnel should be notified well ahead of the tour. Check that plant conditions will not cause any interruptions on the tour. Be sure that appropriate personnel and equipment are available if demonstrations are to be included as part of the tour. Walk through the plant at least once and make sure that you are able to follow the planned route again on your own. Carefully estimate the timing of the tour, including leaving time for contingencies.

Prepare

Notify your learners in advance that they will be going on a tour. Brief them on the purpose of the tour and what will be seen and accomplished. Ensure that all of your learners have appropriate access and coordinate timing with plant personnel. Provide transportation if required.

Tour

Keep on track. Do not allow learners to sidetrack the class. Do not compete with noise interference such as pagers, worker conversation, or background noise—plan for it if possible. Show the actual location and characteristics of individual pieces of equipment. Ask your learners questions and allow them to ask questions.

Follow-Up

You should also meet back in the classroom. Review what was accomplished on the tour. Ask questions to reinforce the experience and ensure the objectives were achieved.

One-on-One Skills Training

Initially, your learner is trained to perform some of the simple operations involved in the job, either in the classroom and/or laboratory, or on-the-job. As the training continues and simple skills are mastered, more advanced operations are added by the master or supervisor in a continual development of skills. Over a period of time, the range of learners' skills is expanded until they are able to perform all of the tasks involved in the total job operation in the proper order and at the proper time.

One-on-one skills training involves not only motor skills training; it is, and should be, supplemented with formal classroom training in both related information and skills acquisition. One-on-one skills training can, and usually does, go on at all levels of an organization from unskilled, entry-level workers to high-level managers. Do not view one-on-one skills training solely as a method to teach motor skills; there is a need for improving the on-the-job learning experiences of all individuals within the organization.

To conduct training for a particular job in the actual work environment is potentially one of the most effective methods for transmitting necessary job skills to a new or inexperienced employee. Often, the real does not match the ideal. One-on-one skills training, like any training, will be effective only to the degree that it is done in accordance with sound learning and instructional principles.

One-on-one skills training has certain advantages as a training method.

- Learning by doing (maximum involvement) is provided for.
- Since the learning environment is the working environment, the transfer of learning is simple and natural.
- The operation may be performed many times for maximum practice.
- Performance and progress are constantly under review by the instructor.
- Feedback is immediate.
- Progress can easily be seen.

One-on-one skills training also has some disadvantages. These exist even in planned and properly conducted training.

- Your learner can sometimes be overwhelmed by what appears to be an impossible learning task. This occurs because the entire operation is what is most apparent; smaller steps are not as obvious.
- The training process is extended over a longer period of time than with other training methods.
- Any mistakes made by an instructor (master) can negatively affect the quality and the quantity of the work group's performance.
- Only a limited number of individuals can be trained at one time by one instructor.

Techniques for Successful One-on-One Skills Training

When preparing for one-on-one skills training, remember the four-step training method for skills training.

- PREPARE yourself to instruct and your learner to receive the instruction.
- PRESENT the operation to your learner.
- APPLY the learning in practice sessions.
- EVALUATE the performance.

Remember to follow-up, correcting and reinforcing as necessary. This may mean retraining the learners or redesigning the training, based on learner feedback.

When conducting one-on-one skills training you should carry out the following preparations:

- Prepare and review skills checklists (lesson plans) and standards to ensure expectations are clearly understood.
- Break the job down into its smaller elements. To do this, write down, in order, all of the steps involved that require explanation and/or demonstration to your learner. Plan to take your learner from simple elements to more complex elements.
- Prepare a training timetable showing what part of the workday you will spend and how long you expect the learning of each job element to take.
- Prepare the work area where your training will take place. It is your responsibility to see to it that all necessary tools, equipment, and materials are readily available. Take whatever safety precautions are necessary to protect the trainee.

When preparing your learner:

- Put your learner at ease.
- Determine what is already known about the job.
- Motivate and encourage your learner.

When presenting the instruction:

- Explain and demonstrate each operation. Be patient! Remember this is new to your learner.
- Stress and reinforce important steps.
- Explain safety and legal aspects of each operation.

Note: Try not to exceed the amount of instruction the learner can master at one time. If you go too far too fast, you will be "sowing the seeds of frustration."

When observing applications of the instruction:

- Ask questions and have your learner demonstrate the new skill and/or ability.
- Be sure each element has been mastered before going on to the next.
- Provide meaningful job assignments which make use of all the skills the learner has learned up to that time.

When evaluating the skill:

- Closely observe your learner's performance of the job or parts of the job.
- Ask your learner to explain and demonstrate each element to you.
- Correct errors and reinforce the correct method.
- Record performance.

Follow-Up: When the training is complete and your learner is ready to perform the job on her or his own, inform your learner that the training objectives have been met, and the learner is ready to take over the job on a full-time basis. The supervisor's responsibilities, however, are not over. The supervisor must continue to check work habits, correcting and reinforcing when necessary, until the employee functions effectively with only normal supervision. Remember that formal classroom training will never replace the effectiveness of one-on-one skills-training. It only augments the training program.

Apprenticeship

Apprenticeship is a formal, structured workplace training and education program in which your learners participate for a fixed period of time after being hired. After completion of this training, the learner will advance to journeyman status. The structured training and education may include supervised on-the-job experiences, as well as related classroom learning experiences. These related classroom experiences can either be conducted within the organization or in nearby colleges or schools in cooperation with your learner's employer.

Apprenticeship has been used for a variety of skilled trades, as well as public services areas (police, fire, emergency medical services), management training, accounting, and even medical areas.

Planning for Instructional Activities

Instructional activities, as the name implies, are those activities that meet a specific instructional objective; they complement the instructional methods chosen. These activities are designed for a particular audience and often are included in the practice (application) step(s) of the lesson plan. Or they can provide an introduction to the formal lesson and motivate the learners to receive the content. Instructional activities also allow you to establish yourself as a member of the group and to introduce the learners to each other.

The best learning occurs when your learner is involved. Activities fully engage your learners in the learning process by giving them opportunities to draw on their unique knowledge and experience, thus personalizing the learning process. Activities allow concepts to be approached from new and different perspectives. They provide a creative break, a change of pace which can stimulate participants.

Instructional activities serve to enhance interactions among learners by enabling them to become acquainted with each other and build camaraderie. Activities also can foster desired attitudinal change(s). They often promote that "teachable moment."

There are three essential things to consider when planning an instructional activity: (1) relevancy, (2) manner of implementation, and (3) debriefing. These are detailed below.

Relevancy: Answer the following questions to ensure that an activity is appropriate to the intent of the instruction: What is the instructional objective? How does this activity support the objective? Why is this activity important to the learner? How can I make sure my learner will see the relevance of this activity?

Implementation: In considering implementation first ask: Am I prepared? What equipment do I need? Are the rules clear to the participants? Finally ask: Have I tried the activity to make sure it will work?

Debriefing: Some debriefing of your learners about their experiences with the activity is essential to enable them to process what they have learned and allow you to check if the instructional objective has been met. In addition, through debriefing, you may discover how to carry out the activity more effectively in the future. Questions that must be answered include: Have I provided time for the learners to reflect on the activity? Did I reiterate what my learners should have learned in order to reinforce the main points and ensure that they are on track?

When conducting activities, be sure to take into account the following:

- Ensure that learners know what is expected of them before the activity begins (e.g. they know the rules of the game).
- Be sure your learners are arranged properly (e.g. divided into groups, with partners, etc.).
- Do not force people to get involved.
- Have all necessary materials assembled beforehand.

- Set a time limit.
- After the activity has begun, intervene only when necessary.
- Be spontaneous and flexible.
- Be sure to debrief learners following the activity.

There are many kinds of activities to choose from—to be most effective choose those that complement both instructional content and method. If, for example, learners are to attain competence in performing a certain skill, one of the activities should be to practice that skill. If specific knowledge is the instructional objective, then learners should observe, listen, and be required to apply the information presented. In this way they can relate what they have seen or heard to their own experiences. If the knowledge involves learning a principle, plan an activity that requires solving a problem or applying the principle.

Icebreakers

One common introductory activity is the icebreaker. Icebreakers allow learners to become acquainted with each other and thus serve to reduce anxiety. As icebreakers involve the whole group, they also can build group cohesiveness and provide motivation. Icebreakers usually come at the beginning of a lesson. They can be used to establish you, the instructor, as a facilitator, rather than a lecturer. Examples of icebreakers include:

- Learners interview each other and then each introduces their partner to the class.
- Individuals introduce themselves, describing their hobbies, occupation, etc.
- Learners answer a question. (E.g. "What do you hope to gain from this course?" or "What would you rather be doing today?")

Summary

I have presented the advantages and disadvantages of a number of common instructional methods, many of which are used regularly in training programs. You are invited and encouraged to refer to this chapter often as you make decisions on developing training.

Chapter References

Gagné, R.M. (1977). *The conditions of learning*, 3rd ed. New York: Holt, Rinehart and Winston.

King, S.B., King, M., Rothwell, W.J. (2001). *The complete guide to training delivery: A competency-based approach.* New York, NY: American Management Association.

McClure, R., Johnson, B. & Jackson, D. (2003). *Assessing the effectiveness of a student-centered ollege classroom.* St. Mary's University of Minnesota. (ED 477743).

National Fire Academy. (Undated). Module #12: Don't lecture for more than 30 minutes before you run an activity that involves all students. In *Student manual: principles of instruction.* Emmitsburg, MD: Author.

Ricks, D. M. (1982). "Making the most of the first 20 minutes of your training." In P.G. Jones, Ed. *Adult learning in your classroom.* Minneapolis, MN: Lakewood Books.

8

Internet-Based Instruction: Some Fundamentals

Advancing technology has had a profound impact on curriculum and the delivery of education in its ability to move instruction and learning out of and far beyond the classroom.[1] This new method, distance learning, is a planned teaching/learning experience in which instructors and students are physically separated by for all or part of a course. See distancelearning.wisconsin.edu/about_distance_learning.htm.

This anytime/anywhere instruction is increasingly popular with learners who hold full-time jobs and/or have family responsibilities, and they are fuelling greater demand for this form of learning. These learners find new opportunities for higher education that meet their time and accessibility requirements. Internet-based course delivery is now the standard method of instruction in distance learning, requiring instructors to take into account special factors regarding design and delivery.

This chapter includes basic information on providing education via the internet. It will focus on the fundamentals of course design and delivery from the perspective of the student and instructor, including such factors as course content, computer software, and the internet itself. All of the material contained in earlier chapters applies to online instruction;

---

1 The author thanks Dr. William Waters, Director of Distributed Learning, Pensacola Junior College for his thoughts as a reactor to the drafts of this chapter.

however, there are additional aspects to consider, particularly regarding communication.

Learning Management Systems

So you will be teaching on the internet. Before you begin, some discussion of the basics is in order. Specialized software has been developed to facilitate design and delivery of online instruction. Usually called a "learning management system" or "course management system", these programs incorporate features to assist in general administration (grade book, student tracking, etc.) and manage course content. Popular examples include *WebCT*, *Blackboard*, *Desire2Learn*, *Moodle*, and *ANGEL*.

ANGEL

ANGEL is an internet-based training tool that facilitates the creation of sophisticated World Wide Web-based educational training environments. An ANGEL course is easy to use because of a simple graphical user interface that allows the web-based course to be readily accessible by both the students and the instructor. Students can click on links that allow them to communicate quickly with their classmates and the course instructor, as well as work on mastering course concepts. The ANGEL system is also designed to allow the instructor to customize the course using the ANGEL administration tools.

Some of the tools that ANGEL provides include:
- A course home page that presents summary information about the course at a glance
- Easily configured reports for the instructor
- Automated course assessment tools
- Easy access for students to course-related email, podcasting, wikis, and blogs.

The course conferencing system allows communication among all course participants, including the course instructor

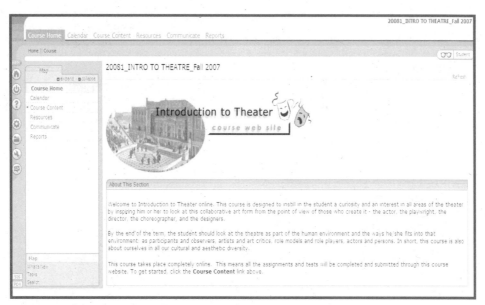

Figure 8-1. An ANGEL Introduction Screen. Reprinted with the permission of ANGEL Learning, Inc.

and students. The conferencing system can be searched for both new and previously posted messages. Furthermore, users can post messages that contain web URLs so that readers can visit relevant web sites.

This program also contains a real-time chat tool to support web-based communication among course participants. Each chat room contains the name of the chat session, the participants who submit comments, their names, and a list of course participants in each room. Figure 8-1 is an ANGEL Introduction Screen.

Learning management systems (LMS) provide various means to manage your course and communicate with your learners, such as:

- chat rooms
- email
- grade book
- student tracking (attendance)

- file management
- links to outside resources, i.e. libraries, online tutoring, etc.

Usually, the firm or school for which you teach will have an instructional technologist on staff to assist you in course design, including the transfer of computer-based content into the LMS, and how to use the LMS itself.

When to Utilize Web-Based Instruction

When should a course be delivered via the internet? This is an important question. Internet delivery of instruction has grown tremendously over the past eight to ten years. As more learners, as well as more people generally, become familiar and comfortable with the internet and its capabilities, more learners want to partake of this kind of learning. Time constraints due to job and family contribute to its popularity, as does the desire to minimize travel to colleges and other schools. Control over one's calendar and environment are advantages. Today's learner has become more comfortable sitting in front of a computer than in a traditional classroom.

Internet-based courses can be asynchronous, that is, the student takes the course at a non-prescribed time with student/faculty communication taking place largely by email, or synchronous wherein learners and often faculty come together to meet online in real-time at an appointed day and hour. The choice depends on the needs of the specific learner populations. Tools and methods for designing internet-based learning are available for both modes of instruction.

As well, online instruction need not be for the entire course. Hybrid or blended courses—those in which some segments are taught traditionally and other parts online—are also growing in popularity.

Who Should Take a Distance Learning Course?

One of the most common statements made about distance learning is that it is not for everyone. So how is the learner to know if a online course and environment is a good match for his/her learning needs and style? Any good distance learning program should provide a tool to determine a student's readiness for online learning. A questionnaire designed to aid the learner and instructor in making these judgments can be found on the Florida Distance Learning Consortium website (www.distancelearn.org/readydl.cfm). Factors to consider include:

Immediacy: Is the learner exploring internet-based instruction because he or she needs to master specific information and has no time to take a traditional school course? Or can the learner take the course in a more traditional classroom at another time?

- Social needs: Does the learner need the support of other learners or can he/she learn in isolation?

- Personal discipline: Does the learner need the continual prompting of others to get things done? Is this person a procrastinator?

- Locus of control: Does the learner take on responsibility readily?

- Time constraints: Considering job and family responsibilities, how much time does the learner have for studies?

- Instructor support: Can the learner work relatively independently?

- Academic history: Is this learner a reasonably successful student, based on past learning history?

Figure 8-2 depicts this questionnaire.

distance.org
Florida Distance Learning Consortium

Home   Course Search   Degree Options   Personal Assistant | Getting Started   FAQs | Contact   Site Map   Login   Search

am i ready for distance learning?

Are online courses for me? Take this quick questionnaire to find out.
Return to the main menu.

1. **My need to take this course now is:**
   - a. High - I need it immediately for degree, job, or other important reason
   - b. Moderate - I could take it on campus later or substitute another course
   - c. Low - It's a personal interest that could be postponed

2. **Feeling that I am part of a class is:**
   - a. Not particularly necessary for me
   - b. Somewhat important to me
   - c. Very important to me

3. **I would characterize myself as someone who:**
   - a. Often gets things done ahead of time
   - b. Needs reminding to get things done on time
   - c. Puts things off until the last minute

4. **Classroom discussion is:**
   - a. Is not necessary for me to understand what I have read
   - b. Sometimes helpful to me
   - c. Almost always helpful to me

5. **When an instructor hands out directions for an assignment, I prefer:**
   - a. Figuring out the instructions myself
   - b. Trying to follow the instructions on my own, then asking for help if I need it
   - c. Having the instructions explained to me

6. **I need instructor comments on my assignments:**
   - a. Within a few days, so I can review what I did
   - b. Within a few hours, or I forget what I did
   - c. Right away, or I get frustrated

7. **Considering my job and personal schedule, the amount of time I have to work on an online class is:**
   - a. More than enough for a campus class or a Distance Learning class
   - b. The same as for a class on campus
   - c. Less than for a class on campus

8. **When I am asked to use computers, VCRs, voice mail, or other technologies that are new to me:**
   - a. I look forward to learning new skills
   - b. I feel apprehensive, but try anyway
   - c. I put it off or try to avoid it

9. **As a reader, I would classify myself as:**
   - a. Good - I usually understand the text and other written materials without help
   - b. Average - I sometimes need help to understand the text or other written materials
   - c. Needing help to understand the text or other written materials

10. **As a writer I would classify myself as:**
    - a. A strong writer - I am comfortable with writing and have strong organizational, grammar, punctuation and spelling skills
    - b. An average writer - I am moderately comfortable with writing and occasionally need help with organization, grammar, punctuation and spelling
    - c. Needing help with my writing, especially with organization, grammar, punctuation, and spelling

11. **I have dropped a college class after the term has started:**
    - a. Never
    - b. Once
    - c. More than once

What's my score?   Reset

Figure 8-2. Reprinted with the permission of Blackboard, Inc. and the
Florida Distance Learning Consortium.

Distance Learning Facts

1. Distance Learning students sometimes can end up neglecting their course work because of personal or professional circumstances, unless they have compelling reasons for taking the course.
2. Some students prefer the independence of Distance Learning; others find it uncomfortable.
3. Distance Learning gives students greater freedom of scheduling, but it can require more self-discipline than on-campus classes.
4. Some people learn best by interacting with other students and instructors, but Distance Learning may not provide much opportunity for this interaction.
5. Distance Learning requires you to work from written directions without face-to-face instructions.
6. It may take as long as two or three days to get comments back by e-mail from your instructor (such as over a weekend or holiday).
7. Distance Learning requires at least as much time as on-campus courses and in many instances up to three times as much.
8. Distance Learning uses computers and other technology for teaching and communication.
9. Printed and/or online materials are the primary source of directions and information in Distance Learning.
10. Distance Learning classes often require written assignments and projects.
11. Students who have dropped a college class often don't have the self-discipline or motivation to work independently and complete an online course.

Scoring

Add 3 points for each "a" that you selected, 2 for each "b", and 1 for each "c". If you scored:

- 28 and over: You may be a self-motivated independent learner and online courses are a real possibility for you.

- 15 - 27: Online courses may work for you, but you may need to make a few adjustments in your schedule and study habits in order to succeed. Online courses take at least as much time and effort and in some cases more than traditional face-to-face classes.

- 14 or less: Online courses may not be currently the best alternative for you. Online courses take at least as much time and effort and in some cases more than traditional face-to-face classes.

Based on IS ELI FOR ME?
© 1989 – 2003, Extended Learning Institute, Northern Virginia Community College. Adapted for this use with permission.

Return to the main menu.

Florida Distance Learning Consortium © Copyright 1997-2004

Figure 8-2, continued.

Technology Requirements & Prerequisite Learning Requirements

What are the technologies and prerequisites for participation in a distance learning course? Prior to registration, information on the exact hardware and software needed, connection speed (56kps or broadband), and any other specific materials required should be made available to students. Learners must be sure that their computers, whether available at home, school, or work, are able to meet these requirements and accommodate their needs. Learners should be familiar and comfortable with such basic tools as email, attachments, chat, and general browser maintenance. They should also be able to use the common non-internet based applications that may be part of a course, such as word processing and spreadsheets. Additionally, learners must be told if prerequisite skills are required, such as completion of a previous course, and this completion must be verified.

Orienting the Learner to the Course

What kinds of information would you wish to have if you were the learner receiving the instruction? You would want to know how the course, or segments of the course to be online, will proceed. Is the course to proceed at the learner's pace? For example, will the learner finish one unit or chapter, take an exam or quiz, and then proceed to the next unit and exam in his or her own time? Or will there be an immediate prompt to go on to the next unit after feedback is provided on the previous unit?

Using a learning management system, the instructor can easily provide a "Start Here" or "Readme First" button/icon that leads the learner to preliminary information on the course. This is the essential information that will help each learner feel comfortable in the online learning environment. In fact, a good instructional design practice for internet-based courses is to provide an initial opportunity for the learner to tour the topics to be learned and mastered, and to learn how to operate within the program itself—how to advance in a unit, how to return to previously covered material, and how to correspond with the instructor and other learners using chat rooms and email.

You should provide your learners with fundamental course information such as:

- *Course Schedule*. The course may parallel a typical academic semester. Or, the course may have a self-paced format in which the learner works on the material at his or her own speed, probably with a fixed final date for completion. All essential dates, such as final exam, final project, etc., must be included.

- *Types of activities and assignments* must be clear. Effective online courses provide opportunities for learners to apply information to practical situations within their individual environments and locales. For, example, a paralegal course might have a learner reviewing a court session in the learner's own town. I once helped design a program in veterinary technology in which learners did an externship within a vet's clinic in their own community. As well, your expectations of the learner's participation in online learning should be clear. Do you see interaction in discussion boards, chat-rooms, and group emails as essential? If so, let the learner know this.

- *Procedures for submitting work* to you, including assignments, projects, self-assessments, and email should be made clear.

- *Assessment methodology.* Many learning management systems have a built-in mechanism for testing. In this case, after the learner completes a fixed unit of instruction, and possibly an applied project, a unit quiz follows. The quiz is then electronically scored with immediate feedback provided or it is electronically transmitted to the instructor for scoring and later feedback. Whatever form of testing is used must be outlined at the beginning of the course. In a formal institutional environment, a proctored or supervised test may be warranted. Learners would be required to report to a central location or campus on an assigned date. Or they might report for proctored testing upon completion of each unit. In any event, these procedures must be made clear to all registering students.

- The biggest problem that learners report with online courses is that of *communication*. Therefore, communications protocols for learners to interface with each other and with you must be established from the beginning. Rules for communication—how learners should conduct themselves in discussion boards, chat rooms, emails, etc.—should be clear.

Figure 8-3 is one example of an internet protocol communications guideline for learners.

As is usual at the opening of a traditional course, an introduction to you, your qualifications, and your general

ONLINE ETIQUETTE = NETIQUETTE
Or
Good Manners While at the Keyboard

DO	DON'T
Use spell check and proofread before hitting the "send" key.	Write grammatically incorrect or incomplete sentences.
Keep the tone conversational but professional.	Use slang, cursing, or excessive abbreviations.
Use upper and lower case letters appropriately.	Use all uppercase letters or all lower case. Uppercase has the connotation of yelling and lowercase is just poor writing.
Make sure you are posting in the correct area of the class (when in doubt, check before sending).	Exchange private emails between two people in public forums like threaded discussion areas.
Put an appropriate title in the subject heading of anything you are sending.	Respond to a post with random or off-the-topic comments.
Use polite language.	Try to use sarcasm--it always sounds more rude than you intended.
Give everyone the benefit of the doubt--we are all learners.	Criticize or poke fun at anyone. Online is NOT private.
Make sure you read and understand your instructor's directions for posting. Each instructor is likely to have infividual requirements.	Assume that all post areas are available for posting. Some areas may be reserved for the instructor to use.

Figure 8-3.

background will be of interest to your learners. This is an opportunity to establish the bond with the learner that is often lost in distance learning. At a minimum, the instructor should present his or her:

- Email address
- Telephone number (office and department)
- Office hours
- Other relevant information of importance

Also, provide an opportunity for the learners to introduce themselves. Using the chat room feature is a good way to do this. And you may gain some insight into how familiar and experienced your learners are with internet-based instruction.

Course Planning and Layout

Planning for instruction is essential to the learner's success in meeting the instructional objectives, as was discussed in Chapter 4. A learner-oriented course environment is necessary and this begins by placing yourself in the learner's place. Realize that internet-based learning can be difficult, as it takes place in isolation, away from face-to-face contact with an instructor and personal support. What would you want in this kind of course in order to be comfortable and have a chance for success?

To facilitate understanding on the part of the student, a learning management system can provide a layout or "course map," a single place where learners can obtain a full picture of the course. This map can include links to organizers, such as a starting point, email, discussion board, course schedule, assignments, quizzes, and even a photo gallery of pictures of students and the course instructor, a means of connecting with the class as a whole.

Internet-based courses should not be simply a collection of written materials electronically filed into a software platform. Rather, the course should be a framework for imparting information in as many different environments as possible. As an electronic aid, the computer allows students to locate and understand information. It should be an embellishment to a classroom experience, rather than only a means of collecting written information.

First, assemble measurable instructional objectives. If you have been teaching the course in a traditional mode, you have your objectives already formulated. They must be measurable. There must be realistic means by which your learners can demonstrate mastery. These objectives must be understood by the learner. Please read Chapter 4, if necessary, to familiarize yourself with the fundamentals of instructional objectives.

The design of instruction for internet-based delivery must facilitate mastery of the specific instructional objectives. Recall from this Chapter that instructional objectives are comprised of four parts: audience, behavior, condition, and standard. Developing internet-based instructional objectives is no different from planning such objectives in any other form of instructional delivery. The key to selecting a process and activity in a well-designed internet-based course lies in the behavior and condition components.

The behavioral component of an instructional objective specifies what the learner must do, produce, or perform in order to demonstrate achievement of the instructional objective. As we design instruction in an internet-based course, we must keep what we wish the learner to master in mind. And this must be conveyed to the learner as part of the course orientation.

Refer again to Figure 4-4 on page . Note the learning capabilities—intellectual skills, cognitive strategies, verbal information, motor skills, and attitudes. Each has specific key verbs. Each has a different performance environment. For an intellectual skill or cognitive strategy, we might design a series of readings that the learner can access via hyperlinks on the computer to read and digest. Alternatively, for a motor skill, we would need to identify manipulative activities away from the computer for the learner to practice and master.

Sample Action Verbs

Capability	Key Verb	Other Possible Verbs	Learning Activity
Intellectual Skills • Discrimination • Concrete Concept • Defined Concept • Rule • High Order Rule	• Discriminate • Identify • Classify • Demonstrate • Generate	• Match, Classify, Combine, Organize • Name, Distinguish, List • Define, Discuss, Reorder, Correct, Outline, Contrast, Compate, Appraise • Solve, Translate, Calculate, Evaluate, Estimate • Synthesize, Explain, Formulate, Create, Improve, Devise	May include esperiential learning activities such as attending a community-based event: theatre production, musical, civic event, etd. connected with the learning topic to observe and apply learning to compare, appraise, synthesize, explain happenings and/or suggest stratebies to improve outcomes.
Cognitive Strategy	• Adpt	• Select, Analyze, Modify, Reorder, Rearrange, Predict, Propose, Plan, Project	Streaming video; Internet-based Text; Hyperlinks to Internet sites.
Verbal Information	• State	• List, Recall, Record	Internet-based Text; Hyperlinks to Internet sites; Discussion Groups via Chartroom
Motor Skill	• Execute	• Manipulate, Tie, Hold, Assemble, Raise, Draw, Knock-down, Operate, Search, Replace, Drive, Twist	Assignments to field-based activities under mentor/proctor supervision.
Attitude	Choose	• Compare, Deside, Act.	Video conference; Internet-based Text; Chat room.

Instructional objectives written to impart attitudinal behaviors can be taught on-line through videoconferencing and chat-room participation. These interactive features enable planned instruction and subsequent feedback to be carried out. Figure 8-4 is one means to incorporate this learning strategy into an online course.

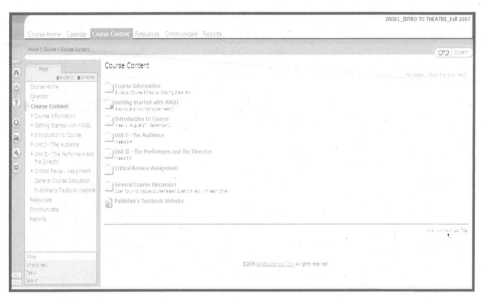

Figure 8-4. Reprinted with the permission of ANGEL Learning, Inc.

Verbal information. An instructional objective to impart verbal information can be accomplished through posting information on the internet, along with exercises completed by the learner either independently or with others in discussion groups. Hyperlinks placed in the text can lead the learner to other sites (e.g., www.lib.utexas.edu/refsites/) that can enhance the learning activity and provide additional information or clarification of the ideas.

1. At the end of this week's lesson, you should be able to identify and/or define the following:

    a. Selectivity
    b. Medium
    c. Characters
    d. Deus ex machina
    e. Ceremony
    f. Ritual

Cognitive Strategies. Cognitive strategies (instructional objectives that contain the action verbs select, analyze, modify, reorder, rearrange, predict, propose, plan) require more elaborate development so as to engage the learner in problem solving and critical skills application. For example, a situation might be presented through a streaming video or pre-planned and developed scenario, after which the learner would be asked to analyze the events and propose solutions. The Introduction to Theatre course mentioned above has a unit in which the stated objectives are:

1. Understand the similarities and differences between performing on a stage in front of an audience and acting before a camera in film or television.

2. Know the three challenges of acting:

   a. To acquire vocal and physical skills that stage performances demand.

   b. To make the characters believable or realistic.

   c. To combine those skills with credibility.

Here the learners are instructed to view selected plays and participate in a discussion board activity as follows:

Discussion Topic for Unit 2:

For this discussion, we will think about and discuss the following:

- If children use imitation and role playing as a way of learning, what effect does what they see in popular entertainment have on their development?

- At what point, if any, do these effects diminish?

- In a society such as ours, which is flooded with the images from popular entertainment, how can children be shielded from negative ideas? Should they be shielded?

- After posting your discussion, please reply to the postings from at least two other students.

For activities, the learners are directed to:

Suggested Plays

- Edward Albee's Zoo
- Leroi Jones's Dutchman
- Eugene O'Neill's Long Day's Journey into Night
- Sam Shepard's Fool for Love

These plays have simple, direct confrontations to point out the dynamic, ever-changing nature of theatre.

Intellectual Skills. Instructional objectives aimed at developing intellectual skills (discrimination, concrete concept, defined concept, rule and higher order rule) are identified by the use of such action verbs as "combine," "organize," "define," "discuss," "reorder," "solve," "translate," "calculate," "evaluate," "synthesize," "explain," "formulate," "create," "improve," and "devise." A multi-sensory approach here is essential. Learners must be cognitively engaged through application of learning and problem solving with immediate feedback. Learners should be presented with a multiple variable scenario via text-based video, hyperlink to alternative site, or other combinations of possibilities.

Motor Skills. To design instructional objectives for such motor skills as the ability to manipulate, replace, and operate is difficult in internet-based instruction. It will be necessary to enable the learner to practice the necessary skills in a controlled and supervised environment, with a preceptor/mentor in charge. For example, in one internet-based course for phlebotomy technicians, learners are sent to a participating medical laboratory that has agreed to provide the required laboratory experiences under the supervision of a licensed phlebotomist technician. The learners are first shown how to locate a vein in a patient's arm and insert the syringe needle and then supervised conducting the procedure a predetermined number of times.

Attitude. To achieve your attitudinal instructional objectives is equally challenging in internet-based instruction. Multimedia is a useful tool. For example, in a course for theatre students, a level of appreciation might be achieved by presenting a series of vignettes incorporating parts of productions that will focus the learners' attention on specific techniques, ideas, and staging. Or if the topic under consideration is theatrical criticism, the assignment for the learner might be to attend a live theatre performance in your area. The post-assignment evaluation could include an oral or written report from the point of view of a critic.

Copyright Considerations

Questions have arisen over the ownership of the product or course developed to convey distance instruction. Much depends on your employment contract. For example, have you devised the course as part of your regular work duties? If so, your employer is usually considered to own the material, according to the US Copyright Act of 1976. However, some institutions and state courts have interpreted this law in such a way as to result in different arrangements. Therefore, a discussion with your institution and/or employer and a written agreement prior to developing a distance learning course with its associated materials is a good idea. For further discussion of these issues, see Primo, et al., (2001) and Lang (1998).

Accommodating Special Needs Learners

As distance learning grows, so have concerns about the accessibility for people with disabilities. As a result, policy guidelines have been developed to ensure that technologies are adapted for their use. For example the "Web Accessibility Initiative" includes guidelines for web content, authoring tools, user agent, and XML accessibility. (www.w3.org/WAI/) Instructors must be familiar with these issues and discuss them with their course instructional designers to ensure learner accessibility.

Other Technologies

- Streaming video: streaming video is a method of delivering video over the Internet in delay-free real-time. An example of one software package that can be used to integrate visual information with textual and verbal information to produce vignettes is Camtasia Studio Screen Software. (www.techsmith.com/camtasia)

- Videoconferencing: Two-way or interactive video/audio discussion can occur over the Internet via a personal computer. This technology often uses proprietary software.

- Embedded graphics are a useful tool and include applications programs such as PowerPoint.

Summary

This chapter has discussed the design, development, and delivery of distance learning via the Internet. As this method of learning expands, all instructors must understand and become familiar with the appropriate techniques presented here.

Chapter References

Connecticut Distance Learning Consortium (2006). http://www.ctdlc.org

Lang, Susan (1988). Who owns the course? Online composition courses in an era of changing intellectual property policies. Computers and Composition. 15(2) 215-228.

Primo, L. H. and Lesage, T. (2001, February). Title survey of intellectual property issues for distance learning and online educators. Education at a Distance Journal 15(2).

Techsmith Corporation (2006). Camtasia Studio Screen Software. www.camtasis.com

Pensacola Junior College (2006). www.pjc.edu

University of Wisconsin Distance Learning (2006). distancelearnning.wisconsin.edu/about_distance_learning.htm

9

Motivation Of Adult Learners: Training For Success In Learning

Be a supportive, helpful, and friendly part of the group:
Teach to combat learner-acquired helplessness.

Up to this point I have discussed the principles and processes of instruction for adult learners. This chapter will discuss a less tangible subject—that of learner motivation.[1] To ensure maximum learning, you must focus your learners' attention on the instructional objectives. You must also understand the concept of learner-acquired helplessness—a major factor in the failure of adult learners in the classroom. I will provide you with insights and ideas for capturing and maintaining your learners' attention, as well as suggestions for using contemporary principles of motivation and reinforcement to ensure that your adult learner performs at a maximum level of potential. Recently, Ahl (2006) has provided more insights on the importance of motivation to adult learning.

The Nature of Motivation

Motivation is innate to all living creatures. It is the inner drive that, from birth, causes all of us to act. Part of it is instinctive, while

[1] The concepts and suggestions offered in this chapter come in large part from material used and developed at the National Fire Academy. I wish to thank my colleague Dr. Robert T. Walls, Professor of Psychology at West Virginia University, who was a principal designer of much of the National Fire Academy's Principles of Instruction materials.

another part is an act of overt behavior, rational and deliberate. Thus, sometimes we act impulsively; other times we act as a result of conscious decisions. Much of human motivation is selfish and self-serving. Your role as an instructor becomes one of directing this natural, in-born, self-directed motivation to assist your learner to master the instruction. Rather than assuming responsibility for creating a desire to learn (motivation), you can be more effective by concentrating your efforts on designing the learning environment (external events of instruction) to stimulate that motivation which already exists. This is not an easy job, but will be one of your most important instructional activities. The combination of your lesson preparation and appropriately selected training activities will spark your learners' motivation, and the learning process will become an effective and enjoyable activity for all.

Your task at this point is to harness the persistence and self-directedness of your motivated learners to create the "teachable moment." This term refers to that moment when all of the motivational factors come together. Your learners' eyes will light up, heads turn, ears tune in, and the entire class will appear to come alive. This phenomenon may occur as a result of something you have said or done or because of input from one of your learners. In any case, this is a time when, for a few minutes or so, you must be a facilitator. Your role must be that of a participant, a fellow learner, an equal—not dominating, but rather guiding your learners in discussion and activity. By maintaining this openness and flexibility in the classroom, you will gain your learners' respect. In the resulting climate, maximum channeling of the internal motivation of all your learners will occur.

The following aspects of motivation are especially important to the instructional process, as underscored by the work and writing of King, King, & Rothwell (2001).

Motivation:

- *provides the drive* that sustains the efforts required for learning.

- *is goal-oriented.* It leads individuals to try to solve a life problem, complete a task, or achieve an objective. It is self-directed.

- *is selective.* It determines the choice of activities with which to become involved, and how to accomplish them. It determines priority.

- *provides a framework for learning.* It helps learners organize activities in the most efficient manner and helps them develop a plan.

Using Your Learners' Needs to Enhance Motivation

Meeting learner needs is one way to enhance motivation. Most adults learn in order to address specific needs, solve life problems, or meet challenges. Adults have a host of needs ranging from basic to complex. Maslow organized needs into five categories:

- physiological (food, water, air, sex);

- safety (freedom from physical danger, desire for security/survival);

- social (acceptance, friendship, affection, loyalty);

- esteem (prestige, respect, achievement, recognition); and,

- self-actualization (total fulfillment as a person).

As an effective instructor, you should make every effort to meet as many of these needs as apply to your training situation. For example, when designing the training, you recognize needs by such arrangements as spacing breaks appropriately or providing opportunity for achievement and recognition. Generally speaking, the more successful you are at meeting learners' needs, the more motivated they will be to learn.

Learner-Acquired Helplessness

Adult learners bring to the classroom a desire to learn and a background rich in experiences upon which to build new knowledge and skills. Unfortunately, some of these experiences can act as barriers to effective learning. Beliefs and predispositions based on negative experiences create learner-acquired helplessness (Abramson, Seligman, & Teasdale, 1978 in NFA, undated (a)), which blocks the ability to progress towards new skills and knowledge. For example, statements such as, "Nothing I can do would make any difference," represent feelings of helplessness (sometimes linked to depression, despair, aimlessness, and suicide) that are associated with not trying to learn in the classroom. You must understand this concept, and help your learners acquire a sense of positive self-esteem, and thus a high level of motivation and readiness to learn.

Self-Esteem and Learner-Acquired Helplessness

Learner-acquired helplessness is greatly intensified in learning environments like the classroom. The more your adult learner fails, the deeper and more ingrained the feeling of helplessness becomes. This failure can contribute to (1) a devastating loss of self-esteem; (2) the belief that one is powerless and that events are controlled by luck, fate, and other powerful people; and/or (3) depression and other dysfunctional emotional reactions. At its worst, a "failure chain" can develop in which your adult learner fails at those tasks that otherwise should be performable. You need to be aware that once a chain of failure has been established, your learner may be unable to solve problems that could have been solved before the series of failure experiences. You must be wary of failure chains and ensure that your learner does not experience repeated failure.

Reasons Given for Failure

When an adult learner does fail, that failure is often attributed to some cause. Your learner may rationalize: "This week has just been too busy," or "I'm just stupid," or "I'll never be able to learn this stuff." These rationalizations are part of *personal* helplessness.

Three kinds of reasons given for failure (attributions) are: (1) Internal/External, (2) Stable/Unstable, and (3) Global/Specific (NFA, undated (a)). Examples of these are provided in Figure 9-1.

- *Internal/External* refers to the locus of control of the failure. Failure may be attributed to reasons under the potential control of the individual (internal); or to forces outside the learner's control, such as chance, the weather, or other powerful people (external). An internal reason might be, "I'd lost a lot of sleep"; an external reason could be, "They never give you enough time."

- *Stable/Unstable* refers to lasting and persistent (stable) *versus* temporary (unstable) reasons for failure. An example of a stable reason for failure is, "This instructor is always tough on women." An example of an unstable reason for failure is, "I didn't study as much as I should have."

- *Global/Specific* refers to the breadth and inclusiveness of the perceived reason for failure. Failure may be attributed to something that affects all subjects (global); or to factors affecting only one test or subject (specific). An example of a global reason is, "All the tests in this program are brain busters"; an example of a specific reason is, "That exam was a real loser."

Several combined ways of attributing failure appear in Figure 9-1. Take the learner who said, "I'm just stupid." This is an internal attribution because the reason for failure is seen to reside within this learner. It is a stable attribution because it reflects a pervasive feeling that the stupidity is relatively permanent. It is also a global attribution because it crosses subject matter boundaries. "I flunked the electronics test because I lost my notes" is an internal, unstable, specific attribution. It is internal since this learner is blaming him or herself for the failure. It is unstable since the loss of those notes will not

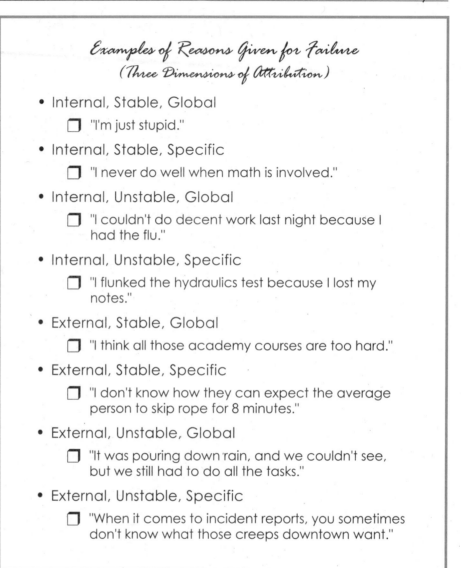

Examples of Reasons Given for Failure
(Three Dimensions of Attribution)

- Internal, Stable, Global
    - ☐ "I'm just stupid."
- Internal, Stable, Specific
    - ☐ "I never do well when math is involved."
- Internal, Unstable, Global
    - ☐ "I couldn't do decent work last night because I had the flu."
- Internal, Unstable, Specific
    - ☐ "I flunked the hydraulics test because I lost my notes."
- External, Stable, Global
    - ☐ "I think all those academy courses are too hard."
- External, Stable, Specific
    - ☐ "I don't know how they can expect the average person to skip rope for 8 minutes."
- External, Unstable, Global
    - ☐ "It was pouring down rain, and we couldn't see, but we still had to do all the tasks."
- External, Unstable, Specific
    - ☐ "When it comes to incident reports, you sometimes don't know what those creeps downtown want."

Figure 9-1.

dictate future failures. It is specific since it concerns only electronics. The external, unstable, global example in Figure 9-1 is dependent on reasons beyond the control of the learner (external); it is dependent on transient weather conditions (unstable); and involves failure on all the tasks (global).

As previously noted, consistent failure can lead to a failure chain and severe feelings of personal inadequacy. Although you should probably be most concerned with the *internal, stable,* and *global* reasons expressed by your learners, any unrealistic attributions are potentially troublesome. For example, a learner who "loses notes" one day, "forgets homework" another day, and "locks books in the car by mistake" another day has a potentially unrealistic attribution problem. Learners who always attribute failure to external causes may be fooling themselves, or they may be secretly feeling internal attributions, but trying to save face. You should help your learners be realistic about the reasons for their failure, but you should also be careful to be sensitive. You *can* assist your learners to avoid potentially detrimental attribution patterns. You *can* help them avoid failure. Repeated genuine and earned success is the key. By providing success experiences for such learners, you can help break the failure chain and quickly stop learner-acquired helplessness.

Instructional Processes to Enhance Motivation

Your responsibility now becomes one of managing both the instructional process and interpersonal relationships in the classroom. The following are specific actions that can be taken to capture and channel a learner's internal motivation.

Establish a Clear Need for the Instruction

Your learners must understand why the material to be learned is important. They must see how they will use the information and/or skills on the job. They also must understand what they will be doing while in training and how they will do it (establish appropriate expectancies). Once your learners understand the reasons for learning specific information and skills (clearly understand the instructional objective(s) of the instruction) and the methods to be used to accomplish the objectives, they will be emotionally prepared to exert the appropriate efforts to be successful at learning.

Demonstrate Enthusiasm and Interest in What Has Been Planned Through Practical Applications of the Material

When you help your learners practice and apply information and skills in a variety of situations (to aid future retrieval and transfer), you are building success chains rather than failure chains. When you help your learners learn to learn, by giving ample examples (selective perception), and practice opportunities, you are promoting transfer (to LTM) of these skills to the real world. When you act as a caring instructor who provides support when and as needed, you maximize the number of successes learners experience. You are, therefore, taking the principles of this chapter seriously. Remember to teach in a way that will combat learner-acquired helplessness.

Present the Proper Quantity of Content Using Varied Methods and at the Proper Pace

You must vary both the instructional methods and activities. Plan appropriate lessons. Use as many methods as possible. Do not fall into a routine and always rely on the same approach. Use audiovisual materials, but do not assume that films or videotapes have built-in motivation. Select those that will be relevant and interesting to the learners on the topic or subject matter that you are presenting. Use examples familiar to the learners. Do not just teach abstract definitions, principles, theorems, or rules, but illustrate these with concrete examples that can be understood by learners.

Plan Activities to Create an Open and Flexible Classroom Atmosphere

Be a facilitator. Get close to your learners psychologically. Numerous authors emphasize the desirability of creating a student-centered learning environment and of an instructor being a member of the group (McClure, Johnson, & Jackson, 2003; Brookfield, 1986; Knowles, 1984). The term "facilitator" has become popular to connote the adult educator as a knowledge broker. These instructors assist learners in identifying resources. They view themselves as participating in a dialogue

---

Recommendations for Getting Close to Your Learners

- ☐ Leave your ego at home.
- ☐ Be with and among your learners physically and psychologically.
- ☐ Get to know all your learners as well as possible.
- ☐ Learn all their names.
- ☐ Often sit with your learners.
- ☐ Talk with a learner as you would a friend.
- ☐ Don't worry about being a "buddy."
- ☐ Remember that respect comes from your competence.
- ☐ Be a concerned knowledge broker.
- ☐ Share your experiences.
- ☐ Be willing to go the "extra mile."

Figure 9-2.

among equally concerned parties. Certainly, as facilitators, they have knowledge of the subject matter that the learners do not, but a spirit of mutual inquiry pervades the helping activities.

Figure 9-2 presents a summary of how to be an open and facilitating member of the learning group. Remember, the effort you make to create this atmosphere of mutual cooperation will be repaid many times over in terms of learner interest, participation, motivation, and recall of the subject matter.

Leave Your Ego at Home

You should talk with your learners and listen to them. Be among them and get close to them. Do not build artificial barriers between yourself and your learners. Sharing your experiences with them without dwelling on "war stories" is a way of being open. There should be a general atmosphere of sharing, flexibility, regard for each other, and openness.

Get Close to Learners Physically and Psychologically

A learner appreciates an instructor who makes the extra effort to help. Be willing to make the extra efforts to help your learner. Caring about your learners and accepting them helps create an open atmosphere. The central elements of trust, mutuality, and purposeful interaction convey the open spirit. The communication concept of immediacy is a key to an open atmosphere in the teaching-learning environment. It helps you to build rapport and become a member-facilitator. In simple terms, immediacy is physical and psychological closeness (McCroskey, Richmond & Stewart, 1986 in NFA, undated (b)), as also discussed in the work of King, King & Rothwell (2001).

If you are competent, this will be clearly apparent with no need for the trappings of superiority. Talk with learners as you would with friends. Do not worry about being too informal with learners. Being friendly will not cause loss of respect. Your respect as an instructor comes from your competence—your knowledge of the subject matter. You are an adult working with adults (Walls, 1987).

Physically, you, as the instructor, should sit with your learners as often as possible. Don't stay behind a desk or lectern. Psychologically, you should get to know something about each learner. Taking the time to talk about, for example, where they work, what they have studied, what they do well, or other similar topics demonstrates interest and creates openness and rapport. Try to learn every learner's name before the second class meets. This takes work on your part, but you will find it worth the effort.

Give Praise Contingent on a Response

"Now, that's the right way to develop that film." Identify specific accomplishments rather than offer only global, positive responses. "Those bearings are tough to get in the right way, but it looks like you got them." Show variety, credibility, and sincerity in your responses, rather than reacting in the same way with little thought. Reward the attainment of an instructional objective, rather than mere participation. "The standard called for 30 seconds and you did it in 12." Help learners compete with themselves and appreciate their own behavior, rather than encourage them to compare themselves with others. "Last time you lost the running end, but this time you nailed it."

Consider how difficult mastery of a task is for a particular learner in your response to individual effort. "Even though you don't have a strong math background, that was accurate and quick." Attribute success to effort and ability, rather than to ability alone or luck or the simplicity of the task. "It takes talent and hard work, but you made it." Help your learners value success in learning rather than in pleasing the instructor. "Pretty soon, you're going to know more about reading blueprints than I do." Provide opportunities for recognition by the instructor and peers. Inform learners frequently of their progress and growth both formally (testing) and informally (verbal feedback).

Promote Constructive Criticism and Provide Confidential Feedback to Your Learners

Be open to constructive criticism and feedback from learners and provide the same yourself. Be flexible; allow for some deviation or redirection to meet learner needs. Offer praise and reward for jobs well done. Provide assistance for training problems. Listen attentively before addressing a concern.

Use learner knowledge and expertise as a learning resource in class. Respect their experience. Be yourself. Be honest. Do not play games. Establish a win/win atmosphere of mutual respect and trust. Make the classroom operate as a team of learners.

Use Nonverbal Communication

Learners pick up many messages through their instructor's tone of voice, facial expression, gestures, posture, and other nonverbal clues (Chapter 3). Remember that both talkers and listeners send nonverbal messages when they frown, smile, look puzzled, cross arms, stare, avoid eye contact, lean back in the chair, turn away, wink, squint, and the like.

Like the behaviors above, the physical distance maintained between people also sends messages. Space speaks. When someone invades our personal space and talks close to our face, it makes us uncomfortable. In our culture, the usual personal distance zone ranges from 18 inches to 4 feet. Casual communication usually takes place in this range. The social distance zone ranges from about 4 to 12 feet. It is usually used by new acquaintances and by those involved in work-related communications. A distance of 12 to 25 feet is sometimes called the public distance zone. It is often used for public presentation and by formal speakers. The intimate distance zone ranges from skin-to-skin contact up to about 18 inches.

Where should you be when you are teaching a class? Here is a general recommendation: occasionally, move within the personal distance zone (18 inches to 4 feet) of each learner; frequently, move within the social distance zone (4 to 12 feet) of each learner. Obviously, this can happen only if you move around. And you cannot be in physical proximity to everyone at once. If you are teaching in a classroom, set it up (if possible) so that you can move down the middle and sides. Set it up (if possible) so that you occasionally can enter the personal distance zone of each learner. Set it up (if possible) so that you frequently can enter the social distance zone of each learner. You will probably be maintaining a public distance zone with most learners if you stay behind a desk or lectern. Get close to them.

Your nonverbal behaviors and those of your learners communicate messages of immediacy, openness, and interest, or the opposite. Research has demonstrated that at least five behaviors are associated with openness and immediacy (Burgoon, Buller, Hale & deTurck, 1984, in NFA, undated (b)). These behaviors let listeners know that the speaker is genuinely interested in what they have to say. Knowing about these behaviors can help you, as an instructor, project your concern for a learner's learning, as well as accurately interpreting feedback from learners.

Receptive and open nonverbal behavior on your part is contagious and helps your learners open up and become more receptive. Thus, in both verbal and nonverbal ways, you should demonstrate that clarity, openness, and respect for others are your guiding principles in communication. Be aware of nonverbal messages but do not over-interpret them. Try to become so involved in helping your learners learn that your body language becomes spontaneous and dynamic in support of verbal messages. Again, *get close to learners both psychologically and physically.*

Provide Opportunities for Early Success: Nothing Succeeds Like Success

Success is the key to motivation because success is what creates motivation. By helping your learners succeed, you become the architect of motivation. The good golfer, the good dancer, and the good card player like to do what they do so well because they are so successful at it. If you have little success at doing something, the pleasure in doing that something soon wanes.

To give your learners as much success as possible, package instruction in easy-to-master pieces so that each person can frequently experience the "thrill of victory." By relating cognitive content to learner experiences and its practical application, and by praising learners verbally and in writing, you help them succeed. Look for ways to give each person in your class the chance to succeed as often as you can.

Catch Them Being Good

Catch your learners being good. Catch them being right. Try to use the "two-to-one success rule" in which you remark on correct responses at least twice as often as you correct them for wrong responses. If you can accomplish this, your learners will work hard, enjoy the course, and remember a great deal of the content. You may have to reward small accomplishments, but always be genuine. Never give phony praise; your skill lies in finding behavior that deserves praise.

Instructors, parents, and people generally often have trouble catching their learners being good. You may say, "One person never does anything right. How can I catch him being good?" Make an effort to find something, even if it is small, and give him some success. Reward him for good behavior and ignore some of the bad. You may be surprised to see what happens. Good instruction will build *success chains,* successful performances based on the learner's expectancy that she or he can succeed. Such chains are built through a process I call *learning-to-learn.* Learning-to-learn consists of cumulative practice with a series of related tasks or problems leading to increased facility in dealing with that general type of task or problem (Biehler & Snowman, 1982, in NFA, undated (c)). As well as providing plenty of practice and problem solving, encourage general transfer of skills by showing how the cognitive strategies can be used in a variety of situations.

Remember, the key to motivation is success. This is the stuff of which motivation is made.

Learn to Use Reward and Punishment Properly

Success results in reward rather than punishment. By definition, reward always increases the likelihood of behavior being repeated. Any stimulus or event that follows a response and increases the future probability of that response may be defined as a reward. If it does not increase the future probability of the behavior that it follows, then it is not a reward. For example, suppose Bill cooked dinner for four consecutive shifts at work. He got a lot of thanks and even a couple of free beers that night when the shift was off duty. They appreciated his work, and he knew it. He felt successful, which increased the probability of his doing the cooking in the future.

Not being successful results in punishment rather than reward. By definition, punishment always decreases a targeted behavior. Any stimulus or event that follows a response and decreases the future probability of that response may be defined as a punishment. If it does not, then it is not a punishment. For example, suppose Bill cooked several meals at work. There were many complaints about the food quality and menu. A couple of people even complained that the food was too spicy. He felt unsuccessful, which decreased the probability of his cooking in the future.

There are two kinds of rewards and two kinds of punishments (Walls et al., 1982). Figure 9-3 provides an easy way to remember them. The behavior under consideration in this figure is "answers a question in class."

An example follows (NFA undated (c)). In Box A, Adam answers a question in class, to which the instructor responds, "That's highly possible." If Adam likes to hear this and considers the consequence of his response to be rewarding (success), the probability of his answering questions will increase in the future.

In Box B, Julie answers a question in class, and the instructor says, "No, that could never occur." If Julie does not like to hear this and considers the consequence of her response to be punishing (failure), the probability of her answering questions will decrease in the future.

In Box C, David answers a question in class, and his buddies in the class start freezing him out and not talking to him. If David does not like to have that companionship taken away and considers the consequence of his response to be punishing (failure), the probability of his answering questions will decrease in the future.

In Box D, Ruth answers a question in class, and the instructor, who has been unpleasant, condescending, and patronizing to her, stops this unpleasant, condescending, and patronizing behavior. If Ruth likes having that behavior taken away and considers the consequence of her response to be rewarding

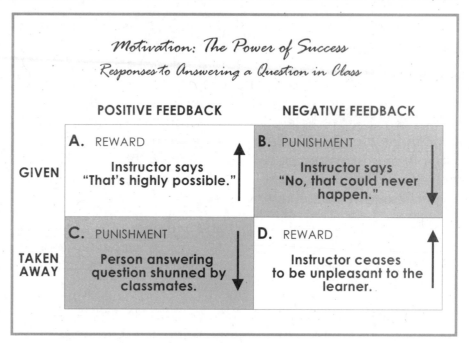

Figure 9-3.

(success), the probability of her answering questions will increase in the future. Thus, in Figure 9-3, in Box A, a positive feedback given after answering a question increases the probability of that behavior in the future (reward and success). In Box B, a negative feedback given after answering a question decreases the probability of that behavior in the future (punishment and failure). In Box C, a positive feedback taken away after answering a question decreases the probability of that behavior in the future (punishment and failure). In Box D, a negative feedback taken away after answering a question increases the probability of that behavior in the future (reward and success).

Thus, giving a positive feedback and removing a negative feedback are two kinds of rewards. Both are interpreted as success by the learner. The two kinds of punishment are giving a negative feedback and removing a positive feedback. Both are interpreted as failure by the learner.

Since success is the key to motivation, reward builds motivation and punishment destroys motivation. As an instructor, you have the power to nurture or kill motivation.

Intrinsic and Extrinsic Rewards

Under ideal circumstances, learning can be its own reward (Biehler & Snowman, 1982, in NFA, undated (c)). Finding the answer to a problem or mastering a skill gives any learner an increased sense of competence. As your learners succeed, you will see a lessening in their need for extrinsic (external) rewards to maintain motivation. As they begin to find the subject interesting, exciting, and satisfying, intrinsic (internal) rewards are sufficient to maintain motivation (Mouly, 1982, in NFA, undated (c)).

Our circumstances are, of course, not ideal. Certainly, as an effective instructor, you want to avoid overemphasis on extrinsic rewards. But, helping your learners to achieve success and understand the importance of that success are crucial instructor functions.

Individualize Assignments or Projects

Remember that a class is composed of different individuals, each with their own needs, goals, abilities, personalities, and interests. Do not use the same plan for everyone in the class. For example, allow learners to choose as many alternatives within a topic as possible for investigation. If the subject matter permits, learners may devise their own projects. In addition, appeal to as many of the senses as possible in planning instruction and selecting media to account for different learning styles. To vary the presentation, invite guest speakers whenever and wherever appropriate.

Summary

Motivation is a characteristic found in every human being. Unfortunately, our learners may not be motivated to do specifically what we want them to do in our instructional setting. To address this difficulty and help them learn, we must strive to meet individual needs and create an atmosphere in which open inquiry can take place.

Chapter References

Abramson, L. Y., Seligman, M. E. P., & Teasdale, J. D. (1978). Learned Helplessness in Humans: Critique and Reformulation. *Journal of Abnormal Psychology, 87,* 49-74.

Ahl, H. (2006). Motivation in adult education: A problem-solver or an euphamism for direction and control. *International Journal of Lifelong Education* 25: 385-405 (EJ739468).

Biehler, R. F., & Snowman, J. (1982). *Psychology applied to teaching,* 4th ed. Boston, MA: Houghton Mifflin.

Brookfield, S. D. (1986). *Understanding and facilitating adult learning.* San Francisco, CA: Jossey-Bass.

Burgoon, J. K., Butler, D. B., Hale, J. L., & deTurck, M. A. (1984). Relational messages associated with nonverbal messages. *Human Communication Research, 10.*

Driscoll, M. P. (1994). *Psychology of Learning for Instruction.* Needham Heights, MA. Allyn & Bacon.

King, S. B., King, M., & Rothwell, W. J. (2001). *The Complete Guide to Training Delivery: A Competency-Based Approach.* New York, American Management Association.

Knowles, M. S. (1984). *Andragogy in action.* San Francisco, CA: Jossey-Bass.

Kuchiuke, K. P. (ed.). (March, 2000). *Academy of Human Resource Development, Conference Proceedings.* Raleigh-Durham, NC, (ED441084).

McCroskey, J. C., Richmond, V. P., & Stewart, R. A. (1986). *One on one: The foundations of interpersonal communication.* Englewood Cliffs, NJ: Prentice Hall.

Mouly, G. J. (1982). *Psychology for teaching.* Boston, MA: Allyn and Bacon.

National Fire Academy. (Undated (a)). Module #15: Teach to combat learned helplessness. In *Student manual: Principles of instruction.* Emmitsburg, MD: Author.

National Fire Academy. (Undated (b)). Module #18: Get close to them physically and psychologically. In *Student manual: Principles of instruction.* Emmitsburg, MD: Author.

National Fire Academy. (Undated (c)). Module #20: Catch them being good. In *Student manual: Principles of instruction*. Emmitsburg, MD: Author.

Walls, R.T. (1987). Being a member of the group. In *Methods and Techniques of Adult Learning*. Emmitsburg, MD: Emergency Management Institute.

Walls, R. T., Haught, P. A., & Dowler D. L. (1982). *How to train new skills: Planning, teaching, evaluating*. Dunbar, WV: Research and Training Center Press.

10

Comprehensive Lesson, Course, and Program Evaluation.

*Help your learners and yourself by evaluating progress
made in achieving instructional goals and objectives.*

Part of your responsibility as an effective instructor is to conduct lesson (or course) evaluations on an on-going basis to ensure adequate planning, content, and delivery. Lesson or course evaluation is often either overlooked or not treated seriously in most training organizations. This chapter describes a process for evaluating the effectiveness of instruction and is based on the assumption that instruction has been designed according to the principles described in previous chapters on instructional objectives and test development.

A Rationale for Evaluation

Lesson evaluation should be performed in order to determine whether:

- the instructional objectives of the lesson meet the job/task analysis requirements;
- learners are able to perform the essential job skills which the lesson or course intended to teach; and,
- your presentation has been effective.

The evaluation process should assess the overall course quality and pinpoint any problems with instructional objectives, content appropriateness (including test items), and your presentation effectiveness. Problems that may be uncovered by this process can include:

- instructional objectives and test items that do not support or are irrelevant to the overall course goals;
- inadequately written objectives, test items, and/or presentation;
- inconsistencies among the instructional objectives, test items, and/or presentations (including your presentation and any associated learner materials);
- instructional objectives that are not reflected in the test items;
- test items that are not associated with any of the instructional objectives;
- instructional objectives (and any associated test items) that are simply nice-to-know or unnecessary;
- inadequate or unsuitable presentation methods, including laboratory exercises; and,
- other problems associated with the training environment.

The Process of Evaluation

Develop Helpful Post-Course Reports

A post-course report serves as a good starting point in conducting lesson or course evaluation. While it may be difficult to make yourself revise a course or part of a course immediately after you finish it, this is the best time to do so. Problems that emerged during your course are then fresh in your mind, and you are more likely to make improvements if you do not delay. Remember to examine and work on fixing only one thing at a time. Even if you improve only one aspect at the completion of each course, over time a great deal of improvement can be achieved.

Thus, when your lesson or course is over, you should immediately assess your efforts. The quality of these assessments helps determine the future quality of the lesson or course and any subsequent revisions that are made. Look at Figure 10-1, the training program post-course report of a typical firm. Developing a helpful post-course report is part of your job as an effective instructor.

One effective and timesaving technique in developing a post-course report is to make notes while your teaching proceeds. As soon as you notice something in class or think of something after class, jot it down on your lesson plan. Note such aspects as typographical errors in lesson plans, errors in handouts, weak writing, poor examples, factual mistakes, sloppy organization, and any other flaws. Also include suggestions for materials that will improve the course. For example, do not hesitate to recommend the selection of a new or a revised overhead transparency or PowerPoint slide, the rewriting of a portion of a lesson, or the inclusion of a new section in the next course. Also, note learner reactions to activities, lesson content, presentation, and questions, as well as to tests or quizzes. Specifically, note any problems learners have with test questions, either in understanding them as written or in their actual responses. Repeated incorrect responses or learner misunderstanding of these questions can indicate poorly written test items, incorrect information, or poor presentation. Write down these comments, as they will be used together with all other evaluation data. Note anything that could improve coordination and operation of the course. Such notes will allow you to write a detailed report in less time.

Just as there is no perfect instructor there is no perfect course. However, improvement is always possible and rethinking what you do is always a valuable exercise. Making a course better is not someone else's job—it is your job as part of a team effort. Build for the future with your course report.

While your post-course report is the first step in a lesson or course evaluation, it must be complemented with a more

Sample Training Program Post-Course Report

Date: March 15

To: Coordinator
               Field Programs Division
               New Milford Police Academy

From: Daniel Gerrard, Treasurer

Course Information:

     Location: Dates:

     Title: Host/Sponsor:

Program Assessment

1. Assistance and cooperation of sponsor/host.

Outstanding. Is an excellent coordinator. My every need
was seen to, most of the time before I knew I needed it. It
is such a pleasure to work with professionals who care so
much about the learners and see to the needs of the
instructor as well. I can't think of enough nice things to
say about the entire group.

2. Adequacy of the training facility and support equipment.
(Include location, arrangement, size, lighting, comfort [ventilation, temperature, chairs, etc.], A/V equipment, and noise level.)

The classroom and the A/V equipment were just fine;
everything that was needed was provided, and was set up
and ready the day before. However, a spare slide projector
bulb should have been available. We needed a replacement
and had to locate a service person during a class break.

3. Adequacy of lodging accommodation and ground transportation.

The motel was just fine, in fact, just what I would have
chosen. The transportation provided was excellent.

4. Cooperativeness of the Field Programs Coordinator.

Is, as usual, excellent to work with. Everything was
handled far enough in advance, and, of course, everything
was on hand in the packet. I certainly look forward to
working with him in the future.

5. General reaction of learners to the Academy course.
(Review content and level—appropriate to learner needs or not.
Report any comments and/or reactions concerning the Academy.)

   The reactions seemed to be favorable; learners liked the course and felt it was of benefit to them. The group seemed to be well selected to meet target group standards. They seemed to get into the course and got a lot out of it. The group appeared to be more comfortable with crowd control processess and procedures than some groups in the past and seemed to enjoy the exercise.

6. Recommendations concerning the course package and delivery.
(Consider content, methodology, group activities, visuals, typographical errors examination questions, etc. Please be specific. Use additional sheets if necessary.)

   On Slide 1-7 "Office" should be "Officer" and "Giver" should be"Given."

   On page 1G 11-21 (J), second paragraph, last sentence reads: "When a senior officer appears on the scene, that officer automatically assumes command." It seems to me that the senior officer would defer assuming command until the incident was under control, or until such time as circumstances warrant it. (See further corrections on attached sheet.)

7. Recommendations to improve Academy planning, scheduling, coordination, and follow up in the delivery of field programs.

   I am well pleased with the Academy field programs.

8. Other comments/suggestions/recommendations

   The COMMAND SEQUENCE still seems a bit bumpy. I am working on some ideas to smooth that section. All in all, it is a good course; I enjoy teaching it. Again, thanks for all the support. I continue to be impressed at how well the Field Programs Division fuctions with such a small staff. It can't happen without your outstanding work.

Figure 10-1.

analytical assessment of your overall effectiveness. Periodically, you should supplement your post-course report findings with a complete lesson evaluation, proceeding first with a thorough review of the instructional objectives supporting the lesson or course. Chapter 4 discussed the use and writing of effective instructional objectives to serve as a "roadmap" for both your learner and you, the instructor. A properly constructed lesson (or course) is based upon soundly written instructional objectives, which specify the desired workplace-documented worker performances (i.e. learner behaviors) in action terms, to specific performance standards, and under specified conditions. The objectives must be reviewed on the basis of the job/task analysis. This will help pinpoint and correct instructional and testing problems.

Additional essential components to be examined in the process of lesson and course evaluation are the test items or means by which your learners are evaluated on their progress through the lesson or course, and the means by which content presentation is evaluated (see Chapter 5). You also need to collect and assess learner feedback. This information, together with a thorough critique of your presentation effectiveness, will provide you with valuable insights into how effective an instructor you have become.

The process that I will describe begins with an instructional objective and test item evaluation to assess lesson design. Next, I will describe a process for presentation evaluation. Finally, I will present a method for collecting and analyzing learner feedback.

An Instructional Objective and Test Item Evaluation

First Clarify and Verify the Overall Lesson or Course Instructional Objective(s)

Review and reflect on each enabling objective of the lesson or course (Chapter 4) by asking yourself, "What should my learner be able to do upon completion of this lesson or course (i.e. does each enabling objective support the terminal objective of the lesson or course)?" "What are the current requirements of the job?" "Have they changed?" All instructional objectives should be directly related to current job requirements.

Now, Complete the Instructional Objective and Test Item Evaluation

Use the Instructional Objective and Test Item Evaluation Form (Figure 10-2) to review and verify instructional objectives. An instructional objective and test item evaluation provides a framework to enable you to:

- first, identify the lesson or course terminal instructional objective(s);
- then, classify all lesson enabling objectives;
- identify essential lesson or course instructional objectives;
- check objective adequacy/appropriateness;
- match test items to objectives;
- check test consistency; and,
- check test and test item adequacy/appropriateness.

To prepare for the lesson (or course) evaluation process make the following materials available:

- all lesson plans and materials containing instructional objectives relating to the lesson or course under evaluation; and,
- all written tests and items and all performance checklists relating to the objectives.

Then, Classify Lesson or Course Objectives

Use a separate form (Figure 10-2) for each terminal objective in your lesson or course. Number each of the enabling objectives (1,2,3, etc.) supporting that terminal objective. Classify each enabling objective as to Remember/Use category (see Chapter 4). Enter the Remember/Use task level in Box "A" on the form. For a "Use" instructional objective, determine if one or more associated supporting instructional objective(s) is (are) necessary and present

Instructional Objective & Test Item Adequacy Evaluation Form

Lesson or Course Title: _____

Terminal Objective Name & Number: _____

Enabling Objectives

Lesson/Course Objective		1	2	3	4	5	6	7	8
Task Level (R/U)	**A**								
Does this objective support the Terminal Objective? (Y/N)	**B**								

Is this Objective:

Essential (✓)									
Nice to know (✓)	**C**								
Unnecessary (✓)									

Appropriateness of Objective:

Conditions (✓)	**D**								
Behavior/Standards (✓)									

Test Item Accuracy

Enter Test Item numbers   □□□ □□□ □□□ □□□ □□□ □□□ □□□ □□□

Does Condition Match? (Y/N)   □□□ □□□ □□□ □□□ □□□ □□□ □□□ □□□

Does Standard Match? (Y/N)   **E**   □□□ □□□ □□□ □□□ □□□ □□□ □□□ □□□

Does Behavior Match? (Y/N)   □□□ □□□ □□□ □□□ □□□ □□□ □□□ □□□

Are Test Items Appropriate? (Y/N)   □□□ □□□ □□□ □□□ □□□ □□□ □□□ □□□

Is Test Item Adequate? (Y/N)   **F**   □□□ □□□ □□□ □□□ □□□ □□□ □□□ □□□

Are there sufficient test items to measure this objective? (Y/N)   □□□ □□□ □□□ □□□ □□□ □□□ □□□ □□□

Figure 10-2.

(answer Yes (Y) or No (N) in Box "B" on the evaluation form). For instance, if the objective is use, unaided, a prior remember-level objective may be needed, especially if the objective deals with a critical use-level performance (see Chapter 4). Review all course objectives and determine the following:

- Is the objective essential (necessary for the job your learners are being trained for)?
- Is the objective nice to know (provides motivation or related information but is not essential for the job)?
- Is the objective unnecessary (unrelated and not needed for job performance)?

Place a check in the Boxes marked "C" on the evaluation form corresponding to your findings.

In performing the above analysis, you should identify and isolate any enabling objectives that have a different training goal from the overall terminal instructional objectives. Previously, you identified the overall course terminal objectives. Now check each essential enabling objective to determine its congruence with the terminal objectives.

Now, Determine if the Instructional Objective is Appropriate and Adequate

The audience, behaviors, conditions, and degrees or standards must be appropriate for the work to be performed either on the job or in later training. Keep in mind the course terminal objective(s). Conditions should be typical of those found on the job. Standards and behavior statements should be appropriate for the work performed on the job. Record your findings of the appropriateness as Yes (Y) or No (N) on the form in boxes labeled "D."

You Should Also Identify the Test Item(s) Associated With Each Instructional Objective.

Using a copy of the test(s) for the lesson or course, identify those test item(s) associated with each instructional objective. If several test items are found for a given objective, each of them will require a separate review. Be sure to identify any instructional objective not tested. If you have more than one test version that contains different questions (not just sequenced differently), match the test questions from all test versions to appropriate objectives. Record your findings on the line provided for test item numbers on the form.

For use-level objectives that require hands-on performance, look for an associated lab exercise. Finally, some test items may not relate to a course objective.

Determine Whether the Test Item Matches the Instructional Objective

Review the conditions under which the test item is administered to see if it matches the conditions in the terminal or enabling objective. Rating scales and performance checklists should also be rated as test items. Review the behaviors called for in the test item against the objective's standard. Record your findings on the form in the indicated boxes labeled "E."

Determine Whether the Test Item is Appropriate and Adequate for the Instructional Objective

I have previously provided for an evaluation of the test item's components: audience, behavior(s), condition(s), and degree(s) or standard(s) to the objective. It may be possible that the test item and objective match perfectly, but the test item may not be appropriate because the objective was not appropriate for the job or training goal. Any test item that failed to meet these previous analyses should automatically be rejected. Referring back to your post-course report, note any items with which your learners had problems. Generally speaking, degrees or standards should become more rigorous and conditions more typical of the job as the learner moves towards a higher training goal.

In order to determine whether the test item is adequate, you should analyze the item (See Chapter 5) in order to address these questions:

- Is the test item clear?
- Is the test item unambiguous?
- Is the test item well constructed?
- Is the test item free of hints?
- Does the test item detect commonly made errors?
- For use level, is the rating scale/checklist well constructed? Are there enough items to test the performance? Are the instructions clear?

Developing test items for instructional objectives that do not require transfer is different from developing test items for objectives that do. A no-transfer objective requires only one or a small number of possible test items. For example, if an instructional objective requires that learners recall the names of the parts of a piece of equipment, the only way to test this is to ask them to recall those parts. Learners should have practiced recalling those names in training. Similarly, if an instructional objective requires performing a procedure on a piece of equipment, the test should require learners to perform that procedure, and they should have practiced that performance during training.

A transfer instructional objective requires a large number of test items. For example, if an objective requires learners to use a rule that applies to a large number of problems, some of these will have been used as examples or practice items during instruction, and others should appear on tests. There will still be many problems remaining that could have been tested and that learners should be able to solve. Since not all test items from this large number can be administered, you need to decide how many test items to include. Learners should be given test items that represent the varying problems that might be encountered on the job. There should be enough test items so that the score learners get on the test accurately represents the score they would get on a test containing all the possible test items, if it were possible to construct such a test. Record your findings in boxes labeled "F."

At this point you have completed the instructional objective and test item evaluation. Now you should proceed to a presentation evaluation in order to ascertain your effectiveness as an instructor.

Presentation Evaluation

This portion of the lesson and course evaluation is carried out by observing you in the classroom or training setting as you deliver the instruction (lesson or course). The observer may be a colleague, a supervisor, or a member of the organization assigned to conduct instructional evaluation. You may be observed over the entire course or a segment thereof. The presentation evaluation will assess your presentation adequacy and consistency, and instructional effectiveness.

Presentation Consistency

The observer will look for:
- inconsistencies between the instructional objective(s) and the presentation;
- instructional objectives that are not present but should be;
- instructional objectives that are present and should not be (e.g. nice-to-know or unnecessary);
- inconsistencies between instructional objectives and test items;
- inadequate presentations; and,
- ineffective presentation, including laboratory exercises.

If, after reviewing the lesson or course, you find any of these problems yourself, or after a more formal evaluation, you should work with more experienced instructors to correct the problems. Remember, the primary goal of the evaluation process is to ensure that the classroom and/or laboratory and/or field instruction is adequately presented and is consistent with the requirements of the job that your learners will be performing.

For a lesson presentation to be consistent with an instructional objective, it must teach to the objective's task level and contain the right combination of presentation components. The five main lesson presentation components must be considered (presented in Chapter 6), and will now be assessed in this presentation evaluation.

The Instructor Evaluation Form, Figure 10-3, is designed to record the presence and completeness of the required lesson presentation components. When considering whether a component is present and complete, evaluate your presentation in the classroom in conjunction with any material, such as your lesson plans. Your lesson plan should be evaluated to check consistency with the objectives. Any learner's guide used is also checked, as it frequently contains practice exercises that learners are required to do as homework. These exercises need to be evaluated to see if they meet the "practice and feedback component" requirements. Also, for courses involving heavily supervised on-the-job training (OJT), a lab exercise can serve as both practice and a test.

Prior to classroom observation, you should identify the instructional objectives to be taught. These objectives should match the numbers assigned on the Instructional Objective and Test Evaluation Form.

Presentation Adequacy

A presentation may include the right combination of presentation components and still not communicate to learners because: (a) the contents are jumbled together in such a way that it is difficult to distinguish one component from another; or, (b) the subject matter requires supporting information or additional explanation to answer learner questions. Other important factors that determine whether or not

Instructor Evaluation Form

Instructor Name: _____	Rating Scale

	weak	average	outstanding

Communication techniques
Clear verbal messages?
Sufficient eye contact?
Appropriate paraverbal message?
Effective interpretation and use of nonverbals?

1 2 3 4 5

Questioning techniques
Questions on overheads used appropriately?
Direct questions used appropriately?

1 2 3 4 5

Introduction to lesson
Gave motivation for lesson?
Appropriate for level of participants?

1 2 3 4 5

Statement of lesson objectives
Formally (written or oral)?
Informally?

1 2 3 4 5

Delivery of information/skills demonstration
Instructor knows subject matter?
Effective presentation?
Information presented in some organized manner?

1 2 3 4 5

Control of classroom environment
Arrangement effective for lesson content?
Presentation aids organized and planned for use?
Control of distractions?

1 2 3 4 5

Use of visual aids
Appropriate A/V choice?
Effective usage?

1 2 3 4 5

Opportunity for application of information or skills
All learners involved?
Sufficient materials for application?
Complete directions for activities given?
Time period for practice stated before activity?

1 2 3 4 5

Evaluation period
Learners advised of evaluation method and occasion?
Measures progress on the objectives?
Valid for the objectives?
Feedback to learners timely?
Informative and developmental?

1 2 3 4 5

Conclusion to lesson presented

Organized and delivered as planned?

1 2 3 4 5

Evaluator_____

Figure 10-3.

communication is effective are included in The Instructor Evaluation Form (Figure 10-3), which is designed to record the findings of the adequacy of each presentation (information) component as follows:

- Your communication skills are effective, including clear voice, good diction, well-paced delivery, sufficient eye contact, and the use of appropriate paraverbal and nonverbal techniques.

- You skillfully use direct, thought-provoking questions to motivate your audience and involve all of your learners.

- Your lesson introduction motivates your learners and sets the pace for the session.

- Lesson objectives are presented to your learners formally either in writing or orally, or both. Objectives are complete and understandable.

- Delivery of information and/or skills demonstration reflects planning and a suitable arrangement of material or content for ease of learner mastery. The delivery follows the lesson plan and effectively uses allotted time.

- Visual aids are appropriate to the instructional objectives and are effectively prepared and used.

- You plan for and appropriately design opportunities for application of information and skills. All participants are involved, with ample time and direction to ensure learner success.

- You effectively control the classroom environment, including presentation media, discipline, distractions, and class management.

- A formal evaluation is conducted with appropriate measures for the instructional objectives. Learner feedback is collected and used for formative assessment of the lesson.

- A conclusion to the lesson is organized, presented, and delivered.

After being formally evaluated through peer observation, you should meet with your evaluator and discuss the findings. Now, plan for action to strengthen any identified weaknesses.

Learner Feedback and Reactions to Instruction

The third component of the lesson or course evaluation process is composed of learner feedback. At the completion of the lesson or course you should provide an opportunity for your learners to formally react in writing to the instructional program. Figure 10-4 presents a typical learner feedback form. It is extremely useful to solicit feedback in the following areas.

- The lesson or course materials, including lesson objectives. Learners should be asked to provide feedback about the adequacy and appropriateness of the instructional objectives. They should also be requested to comment about whether the material actually presented was consistent with the stated objectives.

- The instructional presentation. Learners should be requested to provide feedback about the adequacy and appropriateness of the presentation methodology and media. They should be asked to comment on the clarity of the communication, the usefulness of the teaching aids, the effectiveness of group activities, the opportunity for application of lesson content, the availability of the instructor for help, etc.

- The instructor's demonstrated knowledge of materials and teaching style. Learners should have an opportunity to comment on their perceptions of the instructor's knowledge, as well as instructional planning and proficiency, including reactions to the instructor's ability to convey information in an interesting manner (i.e. using a variety of teaching methods, interacting with learners, handling questions effectively, providing interesting activities, etc.).

- The facilities. Learners should respond to such aspects as comfort in class, access to restrooms, cafeteria,

Sample Learner Feedback Form

		STRONGLY DISAGREE	DISAGREE	UNSURE	AGREE	STRONGLY AGREE	NOT APPLICABLE
1. Printed materials were:							
a. well organized	a.	1	2	3	4	5	6
b. complete enough for me	b.	1	2	3	4	5	6
c. readable (printed well)	c.	1	2	3	4	5	6
d. easy to use	d.	1	2	3	4	5	6
2. Visual materials were:							
a. helpful in understanding the content	a.	1	2	3	4	5	6
b. of good quality	b.	1	2	3	4	5	6
c. in appropriate number	c.	1	2	3	4	5	6
d. easy to see	d.	1	2	3	4	5	6
3. Lead instructor:							
a. related materials to class needs	a.	1	2	3	4	5	6
b. knew subject thoroughly	b.	1	2	3	4	5	6
c. encouraged participation	c.	1	2	3	4	5	6
d. made course expectations, requirements, and objectives clear	d.	1	2	3	4	5	6
e. worked effectively with the adjunct instructor	e.	1	2	3	4	5	6
f. supplemented text with personal knowledge	f.	1	2	3	4	5	6
g. tolerated differences of opinion	g.	1	2	3	4	5	6
4. Adjunct instructor:							
a. related materials to class needs	a.	1	2	3	4	5	6
b. knew subject thoroughly	b.	1	2	3	4	5	6
c. encouraged participation	c.	1	2	3	4	5	6
d. made course expectations, requirements, and objectives clear	d.	1	2	3	4	5	6
e. worked effectively with the lead instructor	e.	1	2	3	4	5	6
f. supplemented text with personal knowledge	f.	1	2	3	4	5	6
g. tolerated differences of opinion	g.	1	2	3	4	5	6
5. The environment included:							
a. comfortable seats and desks	a.	1	2	3	4	5	6
b. efficient handling of registration and administrative details (if applicable)	b.	1	2	3	4	5	6
c. acceptable classroom temperature	c.	1	2	3	4	5	6
d. suitable classroom arrangements/layout	d.	1	2	3	4	5	6
e. sufficient access to required resource materials (if applicable)	e.	1	2	3	4	5	6
f. manageable number of learners in class	f.	1	2	3	4	5	6
6. The course:							
a. contained enough activities	a.	1	2	3	4	5	6
b. included useful activities	b.	1	2	3	4	5	6
c. was a reasonable length	c.	1	2	3	4	5	6
d. covered the right amount of material	d.	1	2	3	4	5	6
e. was worth recommending to others	e.	1	2	3	4	5	6
f. will help me do my job better	f.	1	2	3	4	5	6
g. will be applicable to my job in the future	g.	1	2	3	4	5	6

Figure 10-4.

parking, and seating (taking into account visual abilities of learners), and other relevant matters.

- Materials used in instruction. Learners may comment on access to computers or other tools needed for learning, and library facilities.

- Opportunities for application of new skills and information back on the job. This kind of information from those who took the course will allow you to plan follow-up evaluations of how each learner did once actively back on the job, with input from supervisors.

Summary

This chapter has described the need for and processes involved in lesson, course, or program evaluation. Instructional program evaluation should be performed for several reasons. These include the need to: (1) determine if a lesson's instructional objectives have been met; (2) discover if your learners are able to perform the essential job skills which are the focus of the course or program; and (3) gain valuable feedback about your presentation effectiveness. Evaluation should be approached from the standpoint of congruence of the lesson, course, or program's instructional objectives to the job/task analysis data, learner mastery of the test items, and the adequacy of instructional presentation.

Chapter References

Cantor, J. A. (1986). The Strategic Weapon System Training Program. *Journal of Educational Technology Systems, 14 (3)*, 229-238.

Cantor, J. A. (1987). Evaluation of BVT programs: A systematic model. *The Journal of Vocational Special Needs Education, 10 (1)*, 9-12.

Cantor, J. A. (1988). How to design, develop and use performance tests. *Training and Development Journal, 42 (9)*, 72-75.

Cantor, J. A. (1990, April). How to perform a comprehensive course evaluation. *Performance and Instruction*, 8-15.

Cantor, J. A. (1992a). Evaluation of human performance in critical-skills occupations: Criteria and issues. *Performance Improvement Quarterly, 5* (3), 3-15.

Cantor, J. A. (1992b). Training effectiveness evaluation and the nuclear power industry. A series of articles on development of a measure. A volume edited by Jeffrey A. Cantor. *Performance Improvement Quarterly, 5* (3).

Cantor, J. A. (1992c). Developing multiple-choice test items. A chapter in *The Best of the Evaluation of Training.* Alexandria, VA. American Society for Training and Development, 50-53.

Cantor, J. A. (1996). Developing test and assessment items. A chapter in *The Source Guide for Performance Improvement.* Edited by Kaufman, Roger, T. Thiagarajan & MacGillis. P. San Francisco: Pfeiffer & Co., (Jossey-Bass). 561-584.

Cantor, J. A. (2000, Summer). Industry-sponsored skill certificates and work competency: Establishing a common ground for program design and development. *The Catalyst, 34* (2). 3-7.

Gagné, R. M. (1977). *The conditions of learning,* 3rd ed. New York: Holt, Rinehart and Winston.

11

Learning Environments

Create a learning environment that is collaborative and mutually respectful.

This chapter[1] will discuss those topics relating to learning environments with which you, as an effective instructor, must be familiar: first, managing the learning environment, including learner discipline, and second, selection of instructional media to enhance the learning environment.

Managing Learning Environments

A learning environment is like any other environment, except that it has a special and specific purpose—to foster learning and instruction. Certain instructional materials, physical conditions, and human factors constitute an effective learning environment. Materials include the room itself, and its accoutrements, such as writing boards, chairs, props, overhead, slide, and video projectors, flipcharts, tables, lecterns, and even the wastebasket! Physical conditions include room temperature, ventilation, lighting, size, layout and seating arrangements, noise level, numbers of learners, time of day, and time available for training, as well as available transportation or parking for your learners. Contributing human factors include your skills and abilities as an effective instructor,

---

1 The computer-based instructional technologies section in this chapter was developed by David E. Cantor.

learner attitudes (e.g. motivation regarding the topic), the physiological states and needs of your learners and yourself (enough sleep, food, restroom availability, etc.), and unforeseen interruptions.

A positive learning environment fosters mutual respect and a high degree of trust, and includes recognition of learners' individuality, and learner self-direction and self-initiation. In such a positive learning environment, excellence is valued and effective learning takes place.

A negative environment adversely affects the process and experience of learning. It can decrease motivation, lead to less efficient learning, and/or result in some members of the class learning less than others (e.g. if someone with a vision problem is seated in a visually obstructed location). Each of these negative impacts can be turned into a positive impact by using or improving the learning environment.

As an effective instructor, you must be aware of several key considerations prior to commencing instruction.

Classroom Setting

Room

The room must be appropriate for the kind of instruction taking place. It also must be the right size for the expected number of learners. Breakout (extra) rooms should be available for small group activities. Directions on how to get to the classroom should be available for your learners and other participants. Adequate restrooms and fire exits must be nearby to avoid possible health and safety problems. If any of these are lacking, consider relocating the training elsewhere. Prior to the beginning of the instructional program check the following items. Locate the light switches, and determine that there is adequate lighting for the instructional setting. Also find out where the electrical outlets are. Make sure the room is at a comfortable temperature, and determine whether or not the temperature can be adjusted. Fans should be available if there is no air conditioning.

Seating Arrangements

Before the arrival of your learners, arrange the seating appropriately for the instructional program. Possibilities include: (1) traditional classroom style with seats in rows; (2) seating around a conference table; (3) an auditorium; (4) an U-formation; or (5) a herringbone or chevron (see Figure 11-1). In some cases, it may be appropriate to assign specific seating. In choosing any seating arrangement, consider the maturity of the group, organizational preferences, and the nature of the program. Bear in mind, however, that all seating decisions will affect the learning environment. For example, seats arranged in a circle may encourage freer discussion and class participation than the more formal arrangement of seats in rows.

Parking

Parking is another important consideration when planning for training. If at all possible, ensure that adequate space is available on site for your learners. Make sure that they know in advance where the parking is located. The availability of parking space is often overlooked or simply ignored but, when not attended to, has immediate negative psychological effects on your learners.

Media

You must organize the sequence of events of instruction (lecture, discussion, video or computer presentation, and activities, etc.) and be set up in advance for all such events. Plan sufficiently ahead to ensure that you have obtained the media necessary to support your course or lesson (e.g. flipcharts, visual projectors, and writing boards with markers). Assemble and preview all visuals and media. Ensure that all the machines work and that extra projector bulbs and extension cords are available. Pencils, pens, paper, and other learner

Possible Seating Arrangements for Group Instruction

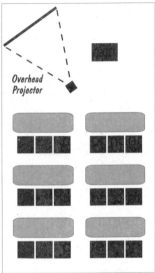

Traditional Classroom

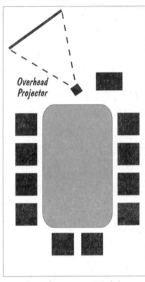

Conference Table

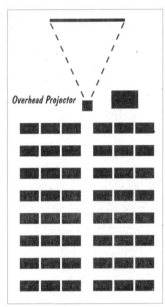

Auditorium

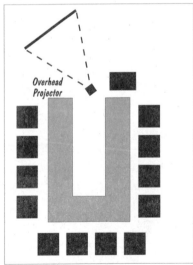

U-Formation

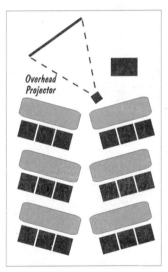

Chevron

Figure 11-1.

materials should be ready for the group. (More about selection and use of media will be presented later in this chapter.)

Class Size

Do you know how many learners to expect? They must be notified as to the time, location, and topics of instruction. Special needs of learners must be identified (e.g. learning or physical disabilities) and arrangements to accommodate them made prior to instruction.

Administrative Concerns

Certain administrative details must be dealt with at the beginning of the lesson or course. These may include such matters as:

- the daily course schedule, including when breaks and lunch will occur and the length of the lesson;
- where the cafeteria or dining hall is located and its hours of operation;
- smoking and all safety (e.g. fire) regulations; and,
- procedures for receiving and making telephone calls, getting mail, etc.

In addition, a final word or two:

- Don't assume anything.
- Preview your facility.
- Have a contact person available for emergencies.

Instructor Liability

We live in a litigious society. As such, instructors must be aware that some of their actions and behaviors could lead to litigation. Commonly, issues that cause liability problems arise in the areas of sexism, racism, rights of privacy (learner records), federal legislation, all items covered by negligence, product endorsement, and copyright infringement. Of these, negligence is most frequently encountered. At its most basic level, negligence is "a lack of ordinary care."

While you should not be overly concerned about your liability risk, bear the following points in mind to avoid liability lawsuits.

- Deal with all of your learners fairly. Use progressive discipline (if, and as needed), and keep adequate written documentation.

- Write instructional objectives carefully and use them when teaching. Keep in mind that your instructional content must reflect best industry practices. Be aware when changes in industry standards dictate changes in your curriculum. Document and record all sources of information and updates on which your course is based. Know why you have included all the information and practices in your course. Preparing your students to perform in a safe and competent manner is the best insurance against litigation.

- Maintain learner records (including lesson plans) and confidentiality about learner performance and grades. Strive to be of benefit to your learner. Respect the confidentiality of student records. Understand that student records of academic progress, as well as their personal information, are only to be accessed and shared by those in the educational institution who have a need to know that information in their conduct of training and school business. Information may not be shared with anyone else, inside or outside of the institution, without the learner's specific permission.

- Be a professional at all times and adhere to industry standards. Act as a reasonable and prudent person would act in similar circumstances. Ensure up-to-date, quality curriculum and proper instruction, supervision, and monitoring of the instructional environment. Having performed as a reasonable and careful instructor, you should be able to defend your position in the case of a legal challenge.

- Provide adequate supervision of learning in laboratory situations. Remember that learners are not masters of the practices being taught and will make mistakes. Be there to prevent injury with its associated litigation. Provide detailed safety and operating instructions on the use of equipment, tools, and processes. Then, adequate supervision and safe environments will ensure proper learning without injury.

- Correct dangerous and defective conditions. Ensure that laboratory and classroom environments are safe and conducive to proper instruction and learning. Never allow learners to work in an hazardous setting. Alert management to all unsafe conditions.

- Finally, to safeguard yourself, obtain adequate professional liability insurance through professional associations.

Problem Participants

There are several kinds of problem learners. This section describes those most frequently encountered, with suggestions for dealing with them.

The Know-It-All

Do not publicly embarrass this learner, but disagree agreeably. Assign the know-it-all a leadership role, or—if this learner is truly competent—let him or her teach a small portion of the class. If this person continues to hinder class progress, discuss the matter privately.

The Talkative Individual

To focus this learner, ask the person to justify any statements with facts and evidence. Another useful technique is to redirect discussion to the rest of the group, using a referred question (e.g. "Thank you, John, for your opinion; now, Bob, what do you think about that?").

The Wanderer

Keep this person on track by glancing at your watch, politely interrupting, and making the person stop. Be courteous, but firm, as you try to redirect that person's attention.

The Griper

Try to determine the basis of the griper's complaints. If the complaint is about something that cannot be changed, tell the person the truth. If something can be changed for the better, allow the griper to research the resolution of the specific complaint.

The Silent Individual

Try to get this person involved in the lesson. Ask this learner to respond to a direct, easy, and straightforward question. Provide reassurance if, and as, needed. Do not seat the silent individual next to a talker.

The Rescuer

Redirect attention to the right person; do not allow the rescuer to protect someone.

If you encounter clashing personalities, play referee. Do not allow a contentious situation to last for too long; emphasize points of agreement. If necessary, call for a break and talk to the participants directly.

The Use of Media to Enhance the Learning Environment

Instructional media can play a vital role in enhancing the learning environment. Media can be thought of as any teaching aids or resources that are used as part of an instructional sequence. Today, the computer has revolutionized teaching and learning. An instructor must understand how computers and specialized software applications work in the training environment to promote and facilitate learning. For the purposes of this chapter, media will be defined as any materials, including computers and computer programs, which are used as adjuncts to demonstrate or clarify course content.

Why Good Media Products are Crucial

Research has demonstrated the effectiveness of using media to: (1) standardize the delivery of instruction; (2) make instruction more interesting; and, (3) shorten instructional time.

The use of media can lengthen the average adult's attention span by strategically refocusing attention (NFAa, undated). It has been estimated that 75% to 95% of what we learn comes through the sense of sight, 10% to 15% through hearing, 3% to 4% through smell, and 1% to 2% through taste and touch. Split-brain research also has implications for media use. The left hemisphere of the brain is thought to be better at verbal processing, while the right hemisphere is supposedly more visually adroit. Further, research indicates that the combination of audio and visual media is more effective than either medium used alone (Anderson, 1983), with learner retention significantly increased over a longer period of time. Thus, the use of media definitely improves both attention and retention.

The Media Selection Process

Selecting the appropriate media for your course, budget, time-table, and learners can present problems. In order to avoid confusion, a selection process outlined by Reiser and Gagné (1983) suggests two important factors to consider when choosing media: ask (1) whether the media are intended as information only or as an integral part of the instruction; and (2) whether the media are intended as the sole source of that particular instruction or are merely aids to instruction. (Refer to Figure 11-2 for classes of media.)

Classes of Media

1. Audio only	Radio Digital recording Teleconference
2. Print	Handouts Flipcharts/Electronic Flipcharts Whiteboard/Interactive Whiteboard Plasma Display

3. Audio-Print	Computer with Audio/Video
	   capability
	DVD or teleconference with print
	   materials

4. Projected Still Visual	Slides Overhead transparencies PowerPoint presentation
5. Projected Still Visual (with audio)	PowerPoint with Internet connection Slides with Internet connection DVD
6. Motion Visual	Computer with Internet streaming video Ipods DVD Movie
7. Motion Visual (with audio)	Computer with Internet streaming video Videocassette DVD Movie
8. Objects	Computeriaed Simulator "Real" things Models
9. Human Resources	Role-plays Field trips Group Discussions
10. Computers	Software Applications

Figure 11-2.

Information or Instruction?

Although an instructor's primary responsibility is to teach, in-house bulletins, special reports, brochures, or other such information presentations may also be distributed as part of the training process. The primary difference between media intended to inform and those intended to instruct is that the former do not require the receivers to demonstrate what they have actually learned from the media. While it is often appropriate to develop and use purely informational messages, remember that any media used for instructional purposes will require that the lesson or course provide evidence of results of using the media.

Instruction or Aids to Instruction?

The distinction to be made here is whether or not the media are to serve as the instruction itself, such as in self-paced courses, programmed instruction, or some computer-based courses. If the media are intended to be the sole source of instruction, rather than just an aid to instruction, or are to be self-paced, they are referred to as an instructional media package. In some cases the media can serve either purpose. For example, a slide-tape program might be used as part of a classroom lesson or for individualized instruction in stand-alone fashion.

If you intend to develop your own visuals, videotape, motion picture, or any other media package that involves both sight and sound, you must use a storyboard. Professionals use storyboards to display visual pictures and related audio script simultaneously. The pictures are mocked-up at one side of the page with the written script for the audio presentation beside them. When making videotapes or movies, it is also a good idea to represent the scene visually on paper with the script beside it.

If the package is intended to be interactive, you need to specify how your learner is to respond. Although a learner response to each slide may not be necessary, you need to insert questions frequently.

Figure 11-3 displays a small piece of a storyboard for a potential unit of self-paced media. The slides are at the left, the tape or written handout script is on the top right, and the learner response is at the bottom right. This piece of storyboard shows you how to get started in making an audio-visual instructional package. If you like to design this sort of instruction or you have a clear need for such a package, first develop a storyboard.

Instructional Aids

Media used as instructional aids are such things as overhead transparencies, slides, flipcharts, graphs, maps, and handouts.

Types of Media

Each of the media has a number of capabilities and limitations. As an instructor, you will be able to decide whether you need to incorporate sound, motion, or color into your demonstration or whether a simple stick-figure drawing will do the job. The types of media are presented here only as a guide; you may want to restructure or add to these categories, based on your own experience, resources, and common sense.

Models and Props

Models and props allow your learners to use several of their five senses in the learning process by observing, handling, manipulating, discussing, and assembling and disassembling objects.

Models are three-dimensional representations of real things, such as engines, human bodies, etc., used to show structure, appearance, or how the object works. There are several types of models: (a) scale models—enlarged or reduced facsimiles in proper proportion; (b) cutaway models (e.g. the inside of an engine that shows the internal structure and the functional purposes and relationships of its working parts); (c) build-up models—sections that come apart and can be put together again to demonstrate parts of the whole and relationship of parts to each other; and (d) mock-ups—three-dimensional

Sample Storyboard Section

Slides

1. Unit Overview
- Major Factors the Incident Commander Must Consider
- Characteristics and Relationships of Factors
- Effects on Firefighter Safety and Survival

2. Major Factors
- Fuel/Fire Load
- Flame Spread
- Heat Transfer
- Flashover
- Backdraft
- Building Construction
- Weather

3. One-Story Office Building

Tape or Handout Script

1. This course considers the "major factors" in Incident Command. From your previous knowledge, see how many of these major factors you can list. The program will pause 30 seconds while you write.

2. These are the seven major factors that an incident commander must consider. The program will pause 30 seconds while you check (and correct, if necessary) your previous answers.

Learner Response

1. Major Factors
   1. _____
   2. _____
   3. _____
   4. _____
   5. _____
   6. _____
   7. _____

2. No response here.

Figure 11-3.

diagrams used mostly in the military and industry which serve to demonstrate, for example, how an engine works. Props are less intricate than models, but are realistic and serve to emphasize instructional points. Both models and props are often expensive and difficult to acquire, but well worth the effort when you are imparting technical information to your learner. They still remain a viable teaching tool today.

Overhead Projectors and Transparencies

Overhead projection transparencies are still a widely used visual aid in lectures, lecture-demonstrations, or other formal classroom instruction. They offer many advantages. The machinery is simple to operate, and developing materials to use with it is easy. The transparencies are inexpensive and very durable and can be used over and over again. They can be generated on and printed directly from your personal computer, using a special acetate film in the paper tray of your printer. Alternatively, they can be prepared in a photocopier, once the original master has been made on regular paper. Variations of overhead projectors are made to interface with computers to project slide shows.

Slides and Slide Projectors/PowerPoint™

Slides are 35 mm pictures, usually multi-colored, and mounted in durable frames. These images can be used again and again, in any order, to bring visual reality into your classroom. When projected by a slide projector, learners can view the slides in a classroom setting, or individually, as a supplement to the classroom lecture. Computer software programs such as Microsoft's PowerPoint™ can be used to prepare slideshows and then show them using a LCD panel or a projector connected to the computer. Powerpoint software enables instructors to create high-impact, dynamic presentations while integrating review workflows and ways to share this information through computer interfaces easily. (http://office.microsoft.com/en-us/powerpoint/HA1016800910 33.aspx).

Videotapes/DVD Technology

Videotapes are very popular supplements to lectures and lecture-demonstrations. Specialty videos are now produced dealing with almost any subject taught in adult training settings, including such areas as emergency medical technician training, law enforcement training, automotive mechanics, etc. DVD technology (commonly "Digital Versatile Disc." and previously "Digital Video Disc") is an optical disc storage media format that can be used for data storage, including movies with high video and sound quality. DVDs resemble compact discs as their physical dimensions are the same (120 mm [4.72 incles] or occasionally 80 mm [3.15 inches] in diameter), but they are encoded in a different format and at a much higher density. As videos come in a number of formats, check the kind of equipment available at your training center or classroom. Videos can sometimes be loaned or rented as well.

When prepared properly, all visual projections allow your learners to take notes, follow main points, and individually pace the acquisition of new information. They focus learner attention on specific items of importance and discussion. Additionally, class handouts can be made directly from these computer-generated graphics so that all your learners can have their own copies for ease of note taking. In delivering lectures or leading discussions, you can easily move graphics back and forth as needed.

Flipcharts/Electronic Flipcharts

The flipchart, usually mounted on an easel, is most useful when a sequence of information (usually involving numerous steps) is to be presented. Flipcharts are easy to use, inexpensive, accessible, and portable. Your learners can participate in the learning process by providing information that will be included immediately on the flipchart. Be sure to write legibly and in large letters. Place the flipchart in the classroom where all the learners can see it. Page turning may disrupt the learning process at times. Electronic flipcharts work like whiteboards with a photocopy capability.

Marking Boards/Whiteboards

Marking boards, or "whiteboards" remain valuable visual aids in lesson presentation. It is accessible and visible to both you and your learners. It is a way to record an ongoing event or one that is changing quickly during the course of a discussion. It enables your learners to: (1) view a process as well as a finished diagram; (2) participate in the analysis and resolution of a problem; and (3) provide suggestions in the learning process. Thus, using the marking board encourages optimum participation from your learners.

The computer and digital technology has now made it possible for digitally transmitting information to the whiteboard via the "interactive whiteboard," which is a whiteboard that is connected to a computer and data projector. Once the computer image is projected on the board, the whiteboard can be used as a computer. The board facilitates instructors and students sharing assignments, editing results and interfacing with and searching the web.

Be careful not to fill up the marking board with too much material. You will want your learners to focus on the points under discussion as you are writing on the board. You may wish to prepare some information in advance, which can easily be hidden from your learners' view by concealing it with a pull-down map or screen (Freedman & Berg, 1967).

Magnetic boards are also a popular addition to the standard marking board. This aid enhances your opportunities to display props, charts, or other audiovisual materials during your presentation.

Development of Media

Once you have chosen the class of media appropriate for your instruction, you begin the task of finding or developing the tool itself. You may be able to find commercially prepared material that will meet your instructional objectives, or it may be necessary actually to create the media yourself. Media development can be a time-consuming process, but good media products that are appropriately related to the instructional objectives yield dividends for your course and your learners. There are some rules of thumb about how big to make the letters on media to be shown on the screen. The best rule of thumb, however, is the "common sense rule." It states, "Make it comfortable to listen to and big enough for everyone to see." In addition, the "2 by 6 rule" states that nobody should be seated closer than two screen widths, or farther away than six screen widths from the projection screen.

Principles of Organization

To prepare overhead graphics, slides, charts, and other media aids, it is helpful to organize your approach based on how people organize their thoughts and perceptions. Five principles to keep in mind are (1) Complexity, (2) Similarity, (3) Proximity, (4) Continuity, and (5) Familiarity (Wiman & Meierhenry, 1969).

Complexity

People organize their thoughts and perceptions according to complexity. Based on research on memory and perception, we know that most people can handle about seven chunks of information at a time (see Chapter 2). In practice, try not to include more than seven (or five or six) chunks of information in the visual display. Sometimes, of course, the subject matter does not cooperate with this recommendation! At the other extreme, do not make your visual so simple that it is trivial (e.g. one word, unless the point that word makes is crucial). Remember that approximately seven chunks of information are about all you should include.

Similarity

People organize their thoughts and perceptions according to similarity. In practice, try to organize your visual aid so that the things you want to be related conceptually appear similar. This can be done with similar colors, shapes or boxes, sizes, or spacing. For instance, the information colored red or put in an oval will be perceived as similar to all information colored red or in ovals and separate from information colored blue or put in rectangles.

Proximity

People organize their thoughts and perceptions according to proximity. In practice, try to put the things you want the learner to group together conceptually in close proximity to each other. The principles of similarity and proximity can work together or at odds with each other. If things that should be grouped together conceptually must be separated spatially, use color or some visual feature to draw attention to their similarity. When the learners must group items that must be quite different in shape, color, and/or size conceptually, put them in close proximity to each other. If you can use both similarity and proximity to plan your visual display, you are making the conceptual impact doubly effective.

Continuity

People organize their thoughts and perceptions according to continuity. We tend to continue our thoughts and perceptions in the direction they are going. This also leads to "closure" of small gaps in our ideas and perceptions. In practice, try to guide the learner in the direction she or he should go by making the information and the art work in the visual both point in the right direction.

Familiarity

People organize their thoughts and perceptions according to familiarity. We organize information around objects and concepts that are familiar to us. In practice, use the familiar to help teach the unfamiliar. Use easy words, simple pictures, and familiar context. This gives the learner the advantage of not having to deal with totally foreign material. It provides a familiar peg on which to hang the new information. This principle of familiarity, along with the others illustrated in this chapter, can help you use media to enhance attention and retention.

Computer-Assisted Instruction

Many computer-based instructional technology tools are available to instructors for use in the teaching and learning process. Some of these tools enable the instructor to better deliver training in the traditional classroom. Others provide a virtual environment in which the instructor does not have to be physically present to assist the learner with achieving a specific learning task, as described in chapter 8.

Computer-assisted instructional technology tools have four potential teaching/learning dimensions. There are: 1) same-time, same-place; 2) same-time, different-place; 3) same-place, different-time; and 4) different-time, different-place. A same-time, same-place environment is one in which the learner and the instructor are able to work together in a shared facility. A same-time, different place learning environment exists when learner and instructor are geographically separated. Sometimes the learner and instructor use the same space but at different times—different time, same-place. A different-time, different-place is an environment in which the learner interacts with the instructor completely virtually (see Figure 11-4).

Same-Time, Same-Place Learning

Instructors traditionally have delivered instruction to learners in a conventional classroom. A growing number of technological tools provide a variety of aids to classroom

	Same Place	**Different Place**
Same Time	• Technology Classrooms • MultiMedia Training Visual Aids • Groupware Technology	• Videoconferencing Systems
Different Time	• Computer-Based Training (CBTs)	• Internet-Based Training Systems

Figure 11-4.

teaching. We can consider three levels of usage of technological aids in the classroom.

Level-1 Technology Classroom

A level-1 technology classroom can be described as an environment that contains the basic technology tools that an instructor would use in a lecture. The types of technologies that are useful here include:

- Whiteboard
- Overhead projector
- Projection system

The whiteboard allows the instructor to draw diagrams, figures, and write key words on the spot. The overhead projector permits the instructor to display transparencies as aids to the presentation. And finally, the projection system allows the instructor to connect to any auxiliary display devices, such as laptop computers.

Level-2 Technology Classroom

A level-2 technology classroom provides a more sophisticated environment in which the instructor has the ability to utilize multimedia presentations. The items needed for this type of facility include:

- Whiteboard

- Document camera
- Multimedia computer
- Multimedia projection system
- DVD system
- VCR system

Standard equipment in a Level-2 classroom would include a computer that has full sound, CD-ROM, and other multimedia capabilities. The instructor may use a program to present lecture materials and other supplementary items, such as animated simulations in the classroom. Additionally, the instructor has the capability of playing videotapes or videodiscs to the students through the use of the VCR or DVD system.

Level-3 Technology Classroom

A level-3 technology classroom contains all of the aforementioned items, and, in addition, provides computers for students so that the teaching and learning process can become more collaborative. The inclusion of computers as a part of the instructional process enables students to interact with one another by submitting ideas and solving educational problems electronically. Some software even allows students to interact anonymously, thereby "leveling" the learning field. This classroom provides:

- Student computers
- A local area network
- An electronic computer link-box system

This environment requires that network technicians set up a computer lab in which the instructor can control the computers from a central workstation and the students' computers connect to a local area network server.

Multimedia Training Visual Aids

For level-2 and level-3 technology classrooms, instructors may find it beneficial to develop and deliver multimedia-training presentations to their students. These multimedia-training presentations can readily be created using a standard suite of office productivity tools. For example, Microsoft Corporation produces the Office Suite ™ that contains:

- Microsoft PowerPoint ™: PowerPoint is a multimedia slideshow program that allows the instructor to embellish lectures and/or use Microsoft's templates to readily construct multimedia presentations.
- Microsoft Word: Word ™ is a word processing program that the instructor can use to construct training supplements and tutorials.
- Microsoft Excel ™: Excel is a spreadsheet program that can be used to demonstrate mathematical and statistical concepts

These programs are interchangeable in that the instructor can formulate teaching concepts using Word and/or Excel and present these ideas to the learner using Microsoft PowerPoint. Similarly, the instructor can produce teaching supplements, such as student guides, to assist in the teaching and learning process by incorporating charts and graphs created using PowerPoint into Excel or Word.

Groupware Technology

In the level-3 technology classroom, some instructors create an electronic environment in which the student collaborates both electronically and anonymously. Instructors have found that students actually learn more effectively and efficiently through a virtual and collaborative environment.

These types of environments can readily be created using special types of software called Groupware technology. Groupware technology can be defined as a software system that allows users to interact through sharing ideas and using team-based problem solving techniques. One groupware product that is being used in the training process is called GroupSystems™. Ventana Corporation manufactures GroupSystems.

Same-Time, Different-Place Learning

With the decreasing cost of videoconferencing technology, more organizations are developing distance education programs to provide educational services to a wider audience. One of the critical components of any distance education program is the use of real-time interactive video, voice, and data collaboration technology. Several different modes of videoconferencing technology allow for this level of collaboration to occur. These modes include desktop videoconferencing, mobile videoconferencing, and fixed-room videoconferencing facilities.

Desktop Videoconferencing Solutions

Desktop videoconferencing enables users to communicate with one another using video, voice, and data telecommunication. For instance, an instructor can be located in New York, and provide instruction to students located in Washington, D.C., using a desktop videoconferencing system. The instructor can load PowerPoint on his or her computer and send the PowerPoint lecture to students located in Washington via a desktop videoconferencing system. The students will be able to follow the lecture completely on-line and raise questions as they occur during the course of the lecture. Of course, the students in Washington will need a compatible system at their location.

The standard desktop videoconferencing system consists of a personal computer equipped with a desktop videoconferencing software package, a video capture card, and a headset/microphone. One vendor that provides the software necessary to begin desktop videoconferencing is Microsoft Corporation. Microsoft sells a product called NetMeeting™ that allows for data, video, and voice collaboration over videoconferencing networks (both TCP/IP and ISDN telecommunication networks). Several vendors provide video capture boards that support desktop videoconferencing. One prominent vendor is Intel Corporation with its Proshare™ videocard line.

Same-Place, Different-Time Learning

Many instructors realize that students find it valuable to use out-of-classroom multimedia training supplements to reinforce concepts covered in their courses. These multimedia training supplements typically are highly interactive and allow the student to work at their own pace on some of the more challenging concepts that were introduced during the initial learning experience. Some of the tools that allow students to learn at their own pace will be described in more detail below.

Computer-Based Training (CBTs)

Computer-based training employs a combination of graphics, text, audio and video presentations prepackaged by training professionals on media such as CD-ROMS. This can make for tremendous savings in costs to companies, as employees no longer have to receive in-person formal training during normal work hours. Rather an employee can receive the same quality of training through the use of a just-in-time training system. The CD-ROMs can be run from the employee's computer workstation.

Computer-based training (CBT) can help you meet your computer training goals quickly and efficiently. It is an effective tool to employ when users are at different levels of understanding and expertise. Beginners can proceed step-by-step as they learn a new software program, while intermediate users can start at the point in a training program that makes sense for their skill level. CBT can increase the trainer's ability to deliver training easily and efficiently to more people in less time. It is an on-demand training system—learners can access quality instruction whenever it is needed. This training also allows students to learn course material at their own pace.

Different-Place, Different-Time Learning

Instructors are finding it very valuable to be able to interact with their students outside of the classroom through asynchronous means (e.g. different-time, different-place). This is being made possible through the Internet Some of the means that instructors are using to communicate with their students include:

- Email
- Listservs
- Discussion newsgroups
- Virtual chat rooms

Some instructors are creating Internet-based training facilities and course-based Intranets as more advanced ways of distributing course information, including homework assignments, problem-solving learning material, and assessment activities. In fact, some instructors are grading students on their level of participation in these course intranets.

Electronic Mail (Email)

Many instructors now require that students obtain an email account in order to receive essential information concerning class requirements. Some instructors even insists that students first submit their questions regarding course material or class problems before scheduling a time to meet with them for office hours. Other institutions conduct their courses entirely via email.

Listservs

A listserv is an email-based electronic bulletin board in which a student or instructor can send an email to the course participants via an email account that will broadcast the message to all of the members of the course. Furthermore, listservs archive all messages sent to the course participants and can be retrieved later by students who wish to review the discussion thread.

Discussion Newsgroups

Discussion newsgroups are similar to listservs in that they allow the course participants to follow different topics of emails that are generated through the duration of their course. However, discussion does not require that students have access to email. Rather the messages are posted electronically to a web site to which all users have access by using a standard web browser. Users can post a general message, reply to a message, or even create entirely different discussion threads.

Virtual Chat Rooms

Another electronic communications tool that instructors can use to assist in the teaching and learning process is the virtual chat room. These facilities are on-line tools that allow students and the instructor to communicate with one another outside of the classroom. Depending on the nature of the course, different rooms for "themes" or forums can be defined so that on-line discussions can be categorized according to specific subjects.

Internet-Based Training

All the technology tools discussed thus far enable the instructor to create a collaborative teaching and learning environment. However, some software packages (or Internet-based training systems) have been developed that contain many of the technology tools just described, but have more developed capabilities that allow instructors to conduct their courses entirely on-line.

Some of the characteristics that make up such a system include:
- Email and calendaring capabilities
- An assessment system
- A discussion system
- Challenge and response security
- Knowledge repository

Chapter 8 discusses Internet-based training in detail.

Should I Use Computer Assisted Instruction (CAI)?

To make a decision on the value of CAI for your learners, you must consider several factors, including your curriculum and instructional needs, as well as the cost of acquiring or developing materials. You will need to address questions regarding relevant instructional factors (Anderson, 1983) as listed in Figure 11-5. If you answer yes to any of these questions, the next step is to determine how to obtain the software programs you need. Drill and practice or tutorial programs are relatively simple to develop, either by brute-force programming or by obtaining and using an authoring language program. Even though authoring languages have done the programming for you and prompt you to enter the content you want to teach, software development is a time-consuming proposition. You will want to consider the payoff in terms of your instructional goals, other methods of presentation, frequency of software use once it is completed, and eventual obsolescence of the material.

If a demonstration or simulation program appears to fit best with your instructional goals, the problem of obtaining software becomes even more complex. Developing these programs requires sophisticated programming skills and a relatively long lead-time for completion. These problems must be weighed against the benefits of using this technology. When the task to be taught involves expensive equipment, is dangerous, or is too time-consuming to perform, the cost of developing the software may prove to be a bargain.

Computer-Managed Instruction

A related use of computers in education is computer-managed instruction (CMI), in which the computer is used to lessen the clerical burdens associated with teaching. Scoring, assigning grades, monitoring individual learner progress, summarizing the results of instruction, and generating reports can all be handled by computer. While CMI is usually

---

Where CAI May Be Appropriate

CAI may be appropriate under any of the following circumstances:

- The course (or unit) is designed to teach discrete skills (drill and practice).
- Individualized instruction is desirable (tutorial).
- The course (or unit) is designed to demonstrate the relationships among concepts (demonstration).
- The course objectives can best be met by having learners manipulate variables to test hypotheses (simulation).

Figure 11-5.

used in conjunction with CAI programs, it is a valuable tool in itself.

Cost-effective applications of CMI can be evaluated using the guidelines in Figure 11-6. All the functions listed in this figure can be done manually, but once an appropriate CMI program is installed, they can be carried out quickly, accurately, and consistently. The numbers of learners you teach, the kind of data you need, the analyses requested, and the number of reports you are required to submit are all factors in deciding whether the initial time and expense of installing a CMI system is justified.

Thus, in this chapter, we have seen that assisting yourself and your learners through CAI requires careful decision making and planning. The course objectives, the availability of program developers (or the money to purchase software programs), and learner and instructor needs all factor into the decision to use CAI. Although they can be costly in time and dollars, CAI materials can add important elements to your course if they are well developed and used appropriately.

Guidelines for Cost-Effective CMI

CMI may be effective when there is a need to:
- summarize learner data;
- store large amounts of course development material (e.g., task analyses, learner performance, test questions);
- cross-reference tasks or subtasks;
- generate learner or class reports.

Figure 11-6.

Summary

This chapter discussed the elements that contribute to a positive learning environment—the materials, conditions, and human factors involved. Materials and conditions include the room itself and its accoutrements. Environmental conditions include climate and ventilation, lighting, number of learners, time of day, time available for training, room size and layout, seating arrangements, and noise level, as well as available transportation or parking for your learners. Human factors include your skills and abilities as an instructor and your learners' attitudes. The chapter also discussed methods to ensure learner discipline. Finally, information concerning instructional media and its selection and use was presented.

Chapter References

Anderson, R. H. (1983). *Selecting and developing media for instruction.* New York: Van Nostrand Reinhold.

Brown, J. W., Lewis, R. B., & Harcleroad, F. F. (1969). *AV instruction media and methods,* 3rd ed. New York: McGraw Hill.

Coburn, P., Kelman, P., Roberts, N., Synder, T., Watt, D., & Weiner, C. (1982). *Practical guide to computers in education.* Reading, MA: Addison-Wesley.

Dyrefurth, M.J. (1991). *Legal responsibilities and their implications for vocational instructors*. Climax Springs, MO: Quality Training Specialists.

Freedman, F. B, & Berg, E. L. (1967). *Classroom teacher's guide to audiovisual material*. Philadephia, PA: Chilton Books.

Hofmeister, A. (1984). *Microcomputer applications in the classroom*. New York: Holt, Rinehart and Winston.

Microsoft Software (2007). Web-page. http://office.microsoft.com/en-us/powerpoint/HA101680091033.aspx.

National Fire Academy. (Undated (a)). Module #9: Use media to enhance attention and retention. In Student manual: Principles of instruction. Emmitsburg, MD: Author.

National Fire Academy. (Undated (b)). Module #6: Assist yourself and your learners with computer-assisted instruction. In Student manual: Principles of instruction. Emmitsburg. MD: Author.

Reiser R. A., & Gagné, R. M. (1983). *Selecting media for instruction*. Englewood Cliffs, NJ: Educational Technology Publications.

Wikipedia, the free encyclopedia. (2007) Web-page. http://en.wikipedia.org/wiki/DVD.

Wiman, R. V., & Meierhenry, W. C. (1969). *Educational media: Theory into practice*. Columbus, OH: Charles E. Merrill.

References

Abramson, L. Y., Seligman, M. E. P., & Teasdale, J. D. (1978). Learned helplessness in humans: Critique and reformulation. *Journal of Abnormal Psychology*, *87*, 49-74.

Ahl, H. (2006). Motivation in adult education: A problem-solver or an euphamism for direction and control. International Journal of Lifelong Education 25: 385-405 (EJ739468).

American Society for Training and Development. (1983). *Models for excellence: The conclusions and recommendations of the ASTD Training and development competency study*. Washington, DC: Author.

Anderson, J. A. (1988). *Communication textbook*. Beverly Hills, CA: Sage, 1-150.

Anderson, R. H. (1983). *Selecting and developing media for instruction*. New York: Van Nostrand Reinhold.

Anderson, R. C., & Faust, G. W. (1973). *Educational psychology: The science of instruction and learning*. New York: Dodd, Mead.

Anderson, C. M. B., & Craik, F. I. M. (1974). The effect of a concurrent task on recall from primary memory. *Journal of Verbal Learning and Verbal Behavior*, *13*, 107-113.

Ausubel, D. P. (1978). In defense of advance organizers: A reply to critics. *Review of Educational Research*, *48*, 251-257.

Baird, M., et al. (1985). Training and the law: What you don't know might hurt. In *The training and development sourcebook*. MA: Human Resource Development Press.

Becker, W. C., Englemann, S., & Thomas, D. R. (1975). *Teaching 2: Cognitive learning and instruction*. Chicago, IL: Science Research Associates.

Bellezza, F. S. (1981). Mnemonic devices: Classification, characteristics, and criteria. *Review of Educational Research*, *51*, 247-275.

Biehler, R. F., & Snowman, J. (1982). *Psychology applied to teaching*, 4th ed. Boston, MA: Houghton Mifflin.

Birnbrauer, H., Ed. (1985). *Handbook for technical and skills training*. Alexandria, VA: American Society for Training and Development, 83-88.

Blank, W. (1982). *Handbook for developing competency-based training programs*. Englewood Cliffs, NJ: Prentice-Hall, 261-374.

Bloom, B. S., Hastings, J. T., & Madaus, G. F. (1971). *Handbook on formative and summative evaluation of student learning*. New York: McGraw-Hill.

Bolles, R. C. (1975). *Theory of motivation*, 2nd ed. New York: Harper & Row.

Braun, F. (1981). *The Strategic Weapon System Training Program Part I—Description*. Paper presented at the 23rd Annual Conference of the Military Testing Association, Washington, DC.

Brookfield, S. D. (1986). *Understanding and facilitating adult learning*. San Francisco, CA: Jossey-Bass.

Brophy, J. (1981). Teacher praise: A functional analysis. *Review of Educational Research, 51,* 5-31.

Brophy, J., & Good, T. L. (1986). Teacher behavior and student achivement. In McWittrock, Ed. *Handbook of research on teaching*, 3rd ed. New York: MacMillan.

Brown, J. W., Lewis, R. B., & Harcleroad, F. F. (1969). *AV instruction media and methods*, 3rd ed. New York: McGraw-Hill.

Burgoon, J. K., Butler, D. B., Hale, J. L., & deTurck, M. A. (1984). Relational messages associated with nonverbal messages. *Human Communication Research, 10.*

Cantor, J. A. (1985). Task evaluation: comparing existing curricula to task analysis results. *Journal of Educational Technology Systems. 14*(2), 157-163.

Cantor, J. A. (1986). The Delphi as a job analysis tool. *Journal of Instructional Development, 9* (1), 16-19.

Cantor, J. A. (1986). The Strategic Weapon System Training Program. *Journal of Educational Technology Systems, 14* (3), 229-238.

Cantor, J. A. (1987, Spring). A systems approach to instructional development in technical education. *Jouranl of Studies in Technical Careers, IX* (2), 155-166.

Cantor, J. A. (1987, May). Developing multiple-choice test items. *Training and Development Journal*, 85-88.

Cantor, J. A. (1987, December). *The design of criterion- referenced tests to support vocational program evaluation*. Paper presented to the American Vocational Association, Las Vegas, NV.

Cantor, J. A. (1988, January). A new dimension in military instructional development. *Performance & Instruction*, 14-20.

Cantor, J. A. (1988, September). How to design, develop, and use performance tests. *Training and Development Journal*, 72-75.

Cantor, J. A. (1988). *Lecture notes: Corporate training methods*. New York: Lehman College, City University of New York.

Cantor, J. A. (1988). The training effectiveness algorithm. *Journal of Educational Technology Systems, 16* (3), 207-229.

Cantor, J. A. (1990, April). How to perform a comprehensive course evaluation. *Performance & Instruction*, 8-15.

Cantor, J. A. (1992a). Evaluation of human performance in critical-skills occupations: Criteria and issues. Performance Improvement Quarterly, 5 (3), 3-15.

Cantor, J. A. (1992b). Training effectiveness evaluation and the nuclear power industry. A series of articles on development of a measure. A volume edited by Jeffrey A. Cantor. Performance Improvement Quarterly, 5 (3).

Cantor, J. A. (1992c). Developing multiple-choice test items. A chapter in The Best of the Evaluation of Training. Alexandria, VA. American Society for Training and Development, 50-53.

Cantor, J. A. (1996). Developing test and assessment items. A chapter in The Source Guide for Performance Improvement. Edited by Kaufman, Roger, T. Thiagarajan & MacGillis. P. San Francisco: Pfeiffer & Co., (Jossey-Bass). 561-584.

Cantor, J.A. (2000a). Higher Education Outside of the Academy. 2000 Report. Vol. 27, Number 7. ASHE-ERIC Higher Education Reports - 2000. The ERIC Clearinghouse on Higher Education. Washington, DC: The George Washington University, Graduate School of Education and Human Development.

Cantor, J. A. (2000b). Industry-sponsored skill certificates and work competency: Establishing a common ground for program design and development. The Catalyst, 34 (2). 3-7.

Cantor, J.A., and Hobson, E. (1981). *The Strategic Weapon System Training Program Part II: Executive steering group's role-SWS Personnel and Training Evaluation Program*. Paper presented at the 23rd Annual Conference of the Military Testing Association, Washington, DC.

Chantler, G., Schneider, L., Jacobs, W., & Kent, K. (1986). *Multiple company tactical operations*. Emmitsburg, MD: National Fire Academy.

Coburn, P., Kelman, P., Roberts, N., Synder, T., Watt, D., & Weiner, C. (1982). *Practical guide to computers in education*. Reading, MA: Addison-Wesley.

Connecticut Distance Learning Consortium (2006). http://www.ctdlc.org

Cross, P. K. (1981). *Adults as learners: Increasing participation and facilitating learning*. San Francisco, CA: Jossey-Bass.

Dick, W. W. and Carey, L. (1978). *The systematic design of instruction*. Glenview, IL: Scott, Foresman.

Donaldson, L., & Scanell, E. (1986). *Human resource development: The new trainers guide,* 2nd ed. Reading, MA: Addison-Wesley.

Draves, W. K. (1984). *How to teach adults.* Manhattan KS: The Learning Resources Network.

Driscoll, M. P. (1994). Psychology of learning for instruction. Needham Heights, MA: Allyn & Bacon.

Dyrefurth, M.J. (1991). Legal responsibilities and their implications for vocational instructors. Climax Springs, MO: Quality Training Specialists.

Emergency Management Institute (1987). *Methods and techniques of adult learning.* Emmitsburg, MD: Author.

Flanders, N. A. (1970). *Analyzing teaching behaviors.* Reading, MA: Addison-Wesley.

Freedman, F. B., & Berg, E. L. (1967).*Classroom teacher's guide to audio visual material.* Philadephia, PA: Chilton Books.

Gage, N. L., & Berliner, D. C. (1988). *Educational psychology,* 4th ed. Boston, MA: Houghton Mifflin.

Gagné, R. M. (1977). *The conditions of learning,* 3rd ed. New York: Holt, Rinehart and Winston.

Gagné, R. M. and Driscoll, Marcy P. (1988). *Essentials of Learning for Instruction,* Needham Heights, MA: Allyn & Bacon.

Gagné, R. M., & Briggs, L. J. (1979). *Principles of instructional design,* 2nd ed. New York: Holt, Rinehart and Winston.

Gagné, R. M., Briggs, L. J., & Wager, W. W. (1988). *Principles of instructional design,* 3rd ed. New York: Holt, Rinehart and Winston.

GPU Nuclear Corp. (1986). *Training for performance: Basic instructor course text.* Parsippany, NJ: Educational Development Section; Training and Education Department, unpublished.

Granito, A. R. (1972). *Fire instructor's training guide.* New York: DunDonnelley.

Hawkins, R. P. (Ed.). (1988). *Advancing communication science.* Beverly Hills, CA: Sage, 16-182.

Heinrich, R., Molenda, M., Russell, J. & Smaldino, S. (2002). Instructional Media and Technologies for Learning, 7th ed. Englewood Cliffs, NJ: Prentice-Hall.

Houston, J. P. (1986). *Fundamentals of learning and memory,* 3rd ed. Orlando, FL: Harcourt Brace Jovanovich.

Hofmeister, A. (1984). *Microcomputer applications in the classroom.* New York: Holt, Rinehart and Winston.

Hunter, D., Gambell, T., & Randhawa, B. (2005, November). Gender gaps in groups listening and speaking: Issues in social constructivist approaches to teaching and learning. Educational Review 57 (3), 329-355.

Info-Line ASTD. (1988). *Make Every Presentation a Winner*. Alexandria, VA: ASTD, 19.

Institute for Nuclear Power Operations. (1982). *Guidelines for technical instructor training and qualifications.* Atlanta, GA.

King, S.B., King, M., & Rothwell, W.J. (2001). The complete guide to training delivery: A competency-based approach. New York, NY: American Management Association.

Knowles, M. S. (1980). Malcolm Knowles on_ "Some thoughts about environment and learning—Educational ecology, if you like." *Training and Development Journal*, February, 34-36.

Knowles, M. S. (1984). *Andragogy in action.* San Francisco: Jossey-Bass.

Kuchinke, K, & Peter, K. (eds.). (2000, March). Academy of Human Resource Development, Conference Proceedings. Raleigh-Durham, NC.

Laird, D. (1985). *Approaches to training and development,* 2nd ed. Reading, MA: Addison-Wesley, 5-43, 281-297.

Lang, Susan (1988). Who owns the course? Online composition courses in an era of changing intellectual property policies. Computers and Composition. 15(2) 215-228.

Lindeman, E. (1982). "An essay on learning." In *Instructor training handbook*. Hunstville, AL: U.S. Army Corps of Engineers, 9-18.

Mager, R. F. (1984). *Preparing instructional objectives,* 2nd. ed. Belmont, CA: Lake Publishers.

McClure, R. Johnson, B., & Jackson, D. (2003). Assessing the effectiveness of a student-centered college classroom. ERIC Research Report (ED 477743).

McCroskey, J. C., & McVetta, R. W. (1978). Classroom seating arrangement: Instructional communication theory versus student preferences. *Communication Education, 27*, 99-111.

McCroskey, J. C., Richmond, V. P., & Stewart, R. A. (1986). *One on one: The foundations of interpersonal communication*. Englewood Cliffs, NJ: Prentice Hall.

Microsoft Software (2007). Web-page. http://office.microsoft.com/en-us/powerpoint/HA101680091033.aspx.

Miller, G. A. (1956). The magical number seven plus or minus two: Some limits on our capacity for processing information. *Psychological Review, 63*, 81-97.

Montague, W. E., Ellis, J. A., & Wulfeck, W. H. (1983). *The instructional quality inventory (IQI): A formative evaluation tool for instructional systems development* (Monograph). San Diego, CA: U.S. Navy Personnel Research and Development Center.

Mouly, G. J. (1982). *Psychology for teaching*. Boston, MA: Allyn and Bacon.

National Education Association. *Code of ethics*.

National Fire Academy. (1987). *Instructors guide: Preparing for incident command*. Emmitsburg, MD: Author.

National Fire Academy. (1989). *Fire service instructional methodology*. Emittsburg, MD: Author.

National Fire Academy. (Undated). *Student manual for the National Fire Academy Course—Principles of instruction*. Emmitsburg, MD: Author, unpublished.

Nihei, K. (2002, March). How to teach listening. ERIC Classroom Guide Report (ED 475743).

Pensacola Junior College (2006). www.pjc.edu

Primo, L. H. and Lesage, T. (2001, February). Title survey of intellectual property issues for distance learning and online educators. Education at a Distance Journal 15(2).

Provus, M. (1971). *Discrepancy evaluation for educational program improvement and assessment*. Berkeley, CA: McCutchan.

Reiser R. A., & Gagné, R. M. (1983). *Selecting media for instruction*. Englewood Cliffs, NJ: Educational Technology Publications.

Ricks, D. M. (1982). Making the most of the first 20 minutes of your training. In P. G. Jones, Ed. *Adult learning in your classroom*. Minneapolis, MN: Lakewood Books.

Robbins, D. M. (1990, October). Trainees know about training trainers. *Training & Development Journal*, 12-13.

Rog, D., & Bickman, L. (1984). The feedback research approach to evaluation. *Evaluation and Program Planning, 7*, 169-175.

Rosenbaum, B. L. and Baker, B. (1989). The trainer as a behavior model. In P. G. Jones, Ed. *Adult learning in your classroom*, 7-8. Minneapolis, MN: Lakeland Books.

Rosenshine, B., & Furst, N. (1973). Research on teacher performance criteria. In B. O. Smith, Ed. *Research in teacher education*. Englewood Cliffs, NJ: Prentice-Hall.

Seiler, W. J., Schuelke, L. D., & Lieb-Brilhart, B. (1984). *Communication for the contemporary classroom*. New York: Holt, Rinehart and Winston.

Silber, K. H. (2002, March). Using the cognitive approach to improve problem-solving training. Performance Improvement 41 (3): 28-36.

Spaid, O. (1986). *The consummate trainer: A practitioner's perspective.* Reston, VA: Reston Publishing, 1-64.

Stufflebeam, D. L., Foley, W. J., Gephart, W. J., Guba, E. G., Hammond, R. l., Merriman, H. O. and Provus, M. M. (1971). *Educational evaluation and decisionmaking.* Itasca, IL: F. E. Peacock.

Techsmith Corporation (2006). Camtasia Studio Screen Software. www.camtasis.com

U. S. Air Force. (1980). *Handbook for AF instructors.* Colorado Springs, CO: Author.

U. S. Army Corps of Engineers. (1982). *Instructional methods.* Washington, DC: Author.

U. S. Department of the Navy. (1976). *Training specifications manual (Naval Air Maintenance Training Group).* Washington, DC: Author.

U. S. Department of Defense. (1975). *Interservice procedures for instructional systems development* (NAVEDTRA 106A). Washington, DC: Author.

University of Wisconsin Distance Learning (2006). distancelearnning.wisconsin.edu/about_distance_learning.htm

Walls, R. T., Haught, P. A., & Dowler D. L. (1982). *How to train new skills: Planning, teaching, evaluating.* Dunbar, WV: Research and Training Center Press.

Wiman, R. V., & Meierhenry, W. C. (1969). *Educational media: Theory into practice.* Columbus, OH: Charles E. Merrill.

Appendix
Kinetics Dictionary

Note: Although the usually accepted interpretations of the following behaviors are cited, remember that any given nonverbal clue must be evaluated (1) with reference to other nonverbal behaviors, and (2) within the context of the situation. Also be aware that cultural background and influences may change the meaning of any given gesture or expression.

Ankles locked:	tension and anxiety
Arms clenched/crossed:	suspicion, doubt, closed and/or negative attitude
Body forward:	readiness, openness, anticipation of something pleasurable
Body slumping:	boredom, disinterest, lack of attention
Body facing toward another:	openness
Body facing toward exit:	feeling trapped, disinterested
Eye contact (direct):	postive, interested, open to interaction
Eyes squinting:	doubt, suspicion, accusation
Eyes open, twinkling:	openness, anticipation, positive attitude
Finger rubbing cheek:	uncertainty, thinking it over
Finger rubbing eye:	doubt, lack of understanding, "I can't see it."
Finger stroking nose:	doubt, negative reaction to what is being said
Finger alongside nose:	evaluating, "I think I see the point."
Foot tapping:	impatience, disgust, boredom
Fist (tightly closed):	aggression, anger
Frown:	frustration, disgust
Glare:	disgust, irritation, reprimand

Hand in pocket (thumb out):	confidence, authority
Hand rubbing back of neck:	bewilderment, uneasiness, thinking it over
Hands on hips:	aggressiveness, anticipation of or readiness to argue, closed or defensive
Hands with palms up:	openness, accepting
Hands locked behind head:	relaxed, reassured
Hand wringing:	tension, anxiety, nervousness, anger, hostility
Hand to chest:	openness, loyalty, acceptance
Head nodding:	positive response, agreement, encouragement
Head tilted:	openness, acceptance
Jingling money (etc.) in pocket:	impatience, nervousness, concern with temporal goods
Legs crossed:	nervousness, defensiveness, tension, closed attitude
Legs draped over chair:	indifference, rejection
Pacing:	nervousness, anxiety
Pointing:	aggressiveness
Rolling eyes:	disbelief
Smile:	goodwill, acceptance (Western cultures); nervousness (Oriental cultures)
Staring:	too much interest, possible hostility
Steepling (fingertips together):	confidence, control
Thumb hooked over belt:	control, often interpreted negatively by others
Tongue out:	concentration, avoidance of something unpleasant or distasteful
Tugging pants:	anticipation, readiness, "Here we go" feeling
Yawn:	boredom, indifference, tiredness

Index

S

T

U

V

W